BELONGS TO:
GERRY WILSON 2/5/13
604-779-7356

Enjoy & PLEASE
RETURN SOME?
DAY. I NEED

TO RE-READ

GOD BLESS.
CERRY

P.S. NOT MY HIGHLIGHTING
Ha! Ha!

Against an Infinite Horizon

RONALD ROLHEISER

Against an Infinite Horizon

THE FINGER OF GOD IN OUR EVERYDAY LIVES

REVISED EDITION

A Crossroad Book
The Crossroad Publishing Company
New York

The Crossroad Publishing Company
481 Eighth Avenue, New York, NY 10001

Copyright © 2001 by Ronald Rolheiser

First published in Great Britain in 1995 by Hodder & Stoughton, Ltd.

Printed in the United States of America

Cataloging-in-Publication data is available from the Library of Congress.

ISBN 0-8245-1965-5

2   3   4   5   6   7   8   9   10   06   05   04   03   02

I dedicate this book to the Oblates of Mary Immaculate,
my religious community, who have taught me
that ministering to the human soul is more important
than writing on paper.

Contents

Preface

To have faith is to see everything against an infinite horizon. That is a useful definition. Faith is not a question of basking in the certainty that there is a God and that God is taking care of us. Many of us are never granted this kind of assurance. Certitude is not the real substance of faith. Faith is a way of seeing things. It is meant to change our eyesight, to take the reality of our lives and all that is in them — everyday work, relationships, family, love, sex, hurt, longing, fidelity, failure, sin, suffering, and death — and set these against the horizon of the eternal and the infinite. What faith does is give us a double vision: When we have the eyes of faith we see a certain divine glow shimmering within the ordinary, just as we see all that is ordinary against a horizon of the eternal. Plato called this "contemplating the divine," traditional religion calls it "the finger of God in our lives," this book will call it "seeing against an infinite horizon."

Whatever the phrase, there is in the lives of every one of us a conspiracy of accidents that might aptly be called divine providence. We have faith when we can see this, when we can read the events of our lives precisely against a divine backdrop. But how is this to be done?

This book is an attempt to develop a vocabulary to help us to do this. It will focus on ordinary events and try to show how these might be seen and spoken of in the light of the infinite, the eternal, God. It is written for believers and for those struggling to believe. For the most part it is written

from a Christian perspective, from that place within the faith
where I find and steady myself, but it can be read too by those
of other faiths and by those struggling to name their own faith
or their agnosticism. It's a pilgrim's book, with special food for
the restless, but it can be read as well by those who are sitting
down, steady in their lives, not discontent in their faith.

Its language and style are deliberately simple and direct.
This, of course, is a risk. It is not easy to be simple without
being simplistic, carry sentiment without falling into sentimentality, express piety without being saccharine, challenge
toward boundaries without being fundamentalistic, be ecclesial without being churchy, be Christian without being
unhealthily denominational, be personal without being exhibitionist, and speak the language of faith and the Christian
tradition without simply repeating the time-tested formulae
of the past. But that is the attempt here. Only you, the reader,
can judge how well or poorly it has been done.

The book owes much to many people. Some of the persons I am most indebted to are referred to in the book. Others
need singling out: The people at Crossroad Publishing Company have been consistently most gracious to me. To them,
I owe a debt of gratitude, a warm one, particularly to Gwen-
dolin Herder, president of Crossroad, who incarnates their
ethos, and to Paul McMahon, who incarnates their patience.
This book is dedicated to the Missionary Oblates of Mary Immaculate, the religious community of which I am a member.
They incarnate many things, and to them I owe the biggest
debt of all. They challenge me daily to have faith, to stay
grounded as a missionary, and to speak the language of the
poor. From them too I draw my daily bread, no small thing.
The book is as much theirs as mine. It is a missionary offering
from us, the Oblates, for those who yearn to be met by God
in the language of the poor.

Chapter 1

Seeing the Creature against the Horizon of the Creator

The Bigger Picture

Once you accept the existence of God — however you define him, however you explain your relationship to him — then you are caught forever with his presence in the center of all things. You are also caught with the fact that human beings are creatures who walk in two worlds and trace upon the walls of their caves the wonders and the nightmare experiences of their spiritual pilgrimage.

— MORRIS WEST, *The Clowns of God*

What's madness but nobility of soul at odds with circumstance?

— THEODORE ROETHKE, *In a Dark Time*

THE INSUFFICIENCY OF EVERYTHING ATTAINABLE

In the torment of the insufficiency of everything attainable we come to understand that here, in this life, all symphonies remain unfinished.

Karl Rahner wrote those words; not to understand them is to risk letting restlessness become a cancer in our lives.

What does it mean to be tormented by the insufficiency of everything attainable? How are we tortured by what we cannot have? We all experience this daily. In fact, for all but a few privileged, peaceful times, this torment is like an undertow to everything we experience: beauty makes us restless

11

when it should give us peace, the love we experience with our spouse does not fulfill our longings, the relationships we have within our families seem too petty and domestic to be fulfilling, our job is hopelessly inadequate to the dreams we have for ourselves, the place we live seems boring and lifeless in comparison to other places, and we are too restless to sit peacefully at our own tables, sleep peacefully in our own beds, and be at ease within our own skins. We are tormented by the insufficiency of everything attainable when our lives are too small for us and we live them in such a way that we are always waiting, waiting for something or somebody to come along and change things so that our real lives, as we imagine them, might begin.

I remember a story a man once shared with me on a retreat. He was forty-five years old, had a good marriage, was the father of three healthy children, had a secure, if unexciting job, and lived in a peaceful, if equally unexciting, neighborhood. Yet, to use his words, he was not fully inside his own life. This was his confession:

> For most of my life, and especially for the past twenty years, I have been too restless to really live my own life. I have never really accepted what I am — a forty-five-year-old man, working in a grocery store in a small town, married to a good, if unexciting woman, aware that my marriage will never fulfill my deep sexual yearnings, and aware that, despite all my daydreaming and the autographs of famous people that I have been collecting, I am not going anywhere, I will never fulfill my dreams, I will only be here, as I am now, in this small town, in this particular marriage, with these people, in this body, for the rest of my life. I will only grow fatter, balder, and physically less healthy and attractive. But what is

> sad in all of this is that, from every indication, I should
> be having a good life. I am lucky really. I am healthy,
> loved, secure, in a good marriage, living in a country
> of peace and plenty. Yet, inside myself I am so restless
> that I never enjoy my own life and my wife and my kids
> and my job and the place that I live at. I am always at
> some other place inside myself, too restless to really be
> where I am at, too restless to live in my own house, too
> restless to be really inside my own skin.

That is what the torment of the insufficiency of everything attainable feels like in actual life. But Rahner's insight is more than merely diagnostic; it is prescriptive too. It points out how we move beyond that torment, beyond the cancer of restlessness. How? By beginning to understand that here, in this life, all symphonies remain unfinished.

The reason why we are tormented is not, first of all, because we are oversexed, hopelessly neurotic, and ungrateful persons who are too greedy to be satisfied with this life. The first and deep reason is that we are congenitally overcharged and overbuilt for this earth, infinite spirits living in a finite situation, hearts made for union with everything and everybody meeting only mortal persons and things. Small wonder we have problems with insatiability, daydreams, loneliness, and restlessness! We are Grand Canyons without a bottom. Nothing short of union with all that is can ever fill in that void. To be tormented by restlessness is to be human.

But in accepting, truly, that humanity we become more easy in our restlessness. Why? Because, as Rahner puts it, in this life there is no finished symphony, everything comes with an undertow of restlessness and inadequacy. This is true of everyone. As Henri Nouwen says: "Here in this world there is no such a thing as a clear-cut, pure joy." Peace and restfulness can come to us only when we accept that fact because it is only then that we will stop demanding that life — our spouses, our families, our friends, our jobs, our vocations and vacations — give us something that they cannot give, namely, the finished symphony, clear-cut pure joy, complete consummation.

LIFE'S INCESSANT LONGING

All life is fired by longing. The simplest of plants and the highest of human love have this in common — yearning, restlessness, a certain insatiable pressure to eat, to grow, to breed, to push beyond self. Yet longing is something that is rarely examined, despite the fact that it lies at the very heart of the soul. What is longing? What does it mean to yearn? What is this insatiable press inside of us to eat, to drink, to make love, to want to be outside our own skins and to want to make ourselves immortal? Mostly it is unconscious, a dark relentless pressure to reach beyond ourselves.

We see this pressure in plants. A friends of mine shares how, after buying a house, he decided to get rid of a bamboo plant in his drive. He cut the plant down, took an axe, and chopped down deep into the earth, destroying as much of its roots as he could. Then he poured bluestone, a plant poison, on what remained. Finally, he filled the hole, where the plant had been, with several feet of gravel, which he tamped tightly and paved over with cement. Two years later, the cement heaved as that bamboo plant began slowly to make its way through the pavement. Its life principle, the blind pressure to grow, was not so easily thwarted by axes, poison, and cement.

There is an incredible power, a blind pressure, to grow in all things living. If you put a two-inch band of solid steel around a young watermelon it will, as it grows, slowly burst that steel.

The life-push outward will have its way. All of nature is incessantly driven to eat, to grow, to breed, to fight for more life. Humans are not exempt. We see this, unconscious still, in the way babies eat and in the hormonal drives of adolescents. There we see a drivenness, impossible to thwart or deny. Life pushes outward, reaches outward, yearns, longs, and pushes. We see it, more consciously, in adult restlessness, in our greed for experience, our hunger for sex, our insatiability, our push beyond chastity, and even our escapes into daydreams, alcohol, and drugs. We are ever the bamboo plant, blindly pushing upward; the baby, unconsciously crying for food.

The earth is ablaze with the fire of God. Part of that fire is burning longing — blind pressure, incessant hunger, relentless hormones, insatiable restlessness, and crying dissatisfaction. People have always had their own ways of trying to explain this.

Many ancient peoples believed that the human soul was a piece of the divine fire that had somehow become disconnected from God, and it was this divine fire blazing within us, trying to return home, that made us restless. For them, we were on fire because our immortal soul was trying to escape from a mortal body. That idea, the soul as divine fire, might strike us as rather naive and dualistic, but it is in fact a beautiful metaphor that captures and soothes the imagination in ways that most analytical psychology never can.

Where it errs is only in its dualism. The fire, the relentless pressure, is not only in the soul; it is in everything else as well. The cosmos is all of a piece. The chemicals in your hand and in your brain were forged by the same furnace, the furnace of the stars. The story of life, body and soul, is written in DNA — and relentless yearning lies just as much in the cosmos and the DNA as it lies in our hearts and souls.

What is it all for? In the end, longing and yearning are not really sightless at all. They may be experienced as blind pressure, driving life to eat its way through drives, food, sex, friendship, and creativity, but they are the Spirit of God, groaning and praying through us.

This is what Scripture is talking about when it tells us that when we do not know how to pray, the Spirit of God prays through us, in groans too deep for words (Rom. 8:26). At its root, all longing is for the fruits of the spirit; all life, all eros, and all energy, blind or conscious, yearns for charity, joy, peace, patience, goodness, fidelity, mildness, and the union that chastity can bring. Whether it's a bamboo plant pushing through a drive, or a baby blindly taking food, or an adult man or woman kneeling in supplication, the yearning is for this.

UNLIMITED LOVE,
LIMITED CHOICES

"Every choice is a renunciation." That is an old philosophical dictum that helps explain why we find it so difficult to make choices in life. It merits meditation because, among other things, it sheds light on our culture's struggle with commitment.

One of the hardest things for any of us to do today is to make a permanent commitment of any sort, especially when it pertains to love and our options in this area. We are more comfortable with temporary arrangements, arrangements which never burn the last exit visa. Thus, many people are comfortable living together, but they resist getting married. We see the same thing, in parallel, in religious life, where many people are comfortable in making temporary vows or promises but fewer and fewer of them are ready to make a lifelong commitment.

What is at the root of this resistance to permanent commitment? Most analysts suggest that the reason is that, today, more and more people have experienced, firsthand, broken situations, have been victims of such situations — broken marriages, broken homes, broken promises — and thus are naturally more skeptical about ever pronouncing the time-honored words: "Until death do us part."

There is a lot of truth in this, and, in one way, our unwillingness to risk making permanent commitments reflects a certain positive growth. We have had our eyes opened beyond a certain romantic naivete. Insofar as this is true, there is a maturity in our caution. To my mind, however, this is not the major resistance to risking permanent commitment. What is? Our incapacity to accept the limits of our own lives, as expressed in that old philosophical axiom: "Every choice is a renunciation."

Every choice is, in fact, thousands of renunciations: if I marry this person, I cannot marry any of the millions of other potential mates; if I live in England, I cannot live anywhere else in this world; if I become a professional athlete, I cannot go to medical school and become a doctor; if I have this, then I cannot have that. The list could go on indefinitely. To choose one thing is always to renounce many others. Such is the nature of choice.

In most areas of our lives, however, we do not feel this so strongly. We choose, and there is not much pain of loss. But this is not as true in the area of love. Here, consciously and unconsciously, we feel the sting of loss, and thus there is more resistance, more reluctance to close off options. It is in the area of love that we find it difficult to accept the limits of life and love. What limits? The limits that come with being an infinite spirit in a finite world.

Plato once said: "We are fired into this world with a madness that comes from the gods and which makes us believe that we are destined for a great love." That is a more pagan way, though a very good one, of saying what Christianity has always told us, namely, that in heart, spirit, soul, and sexuality we are meant to embrace everyone and we are built for that task. We are destined for a great love. Thus our eros is wide, our longing is infinite, our urge to embrace is completely promiscuous. We are infinite in yearning and infinite in capacity. Yet, in this life, what we meet is never the infinite but the finite.

No wonder commitment in love is so difficult. We have all this energy, all this yearning, all this capacity, we have infinity inside us, and, at a point, it all comes down to this, marrying one person — this particular man or woman — with all of his or her flaws and inadequacies, in this particular place and time. Infinity limited by a finite choice. But such is the nature of actual incarnate human love. True human love, beyond the abstract, beyond daydreams, and beyond the grandiosity of somehow thinking that we are a god or goddess who can make love to everyone, is a deeply painful renunciation. But it is a renunciation that has the potential to healthily ground us in reality in a way that, to my mind, few other experiences can. To make a permanent commitment in love, in the particular, is to grow up in a very important way.

Thoreau once said: "The youth gets together materials to build a bridge to the moon or perhaps a palace or a temple. ...At length the middle-aged man [or woman] decides to build a woodshed with them." So too in love. The child sets out to marry everyone in the whole world. The adult decides to marry one person — and that conclusion is particularly privileged in helping bring one to adulthood in love.

ABSENT FROM OUR OWN LIVES

Recently I had dinner with a young man and woman who are close friends of mine. They had been married for less than two years and were expecting their first child. Both had good jobs: he in communications, she in teaching. Their relationship to each other, while perhaps past that highly charged passion of first fervor, was, by every appearance, good, respectful, loving, and easy. By every practical standard, they should have been happy, in a good season of their lives. But that was not the case. Individually, and as a couple, they were quite restless and frustrated, without being able to pinpoint precisely why. They talked about it in this way:

> It's not that we are unhappy; it's just that our lives seem too small for us. We want to do something more significant than what we are doing, to somehow leave a mark in this world. The city we live in, our jobs, our circle of friends, even our relationship to each other and our involvement with the church, somehow doesn't seem enough. It's all too ordinary, too domestic, too insignificant. Life seems so big and we seem so small! Maybe having this baby will change things — bringing a new person into this world is pretty significant, and irrevocable. At least that will be one timeless thing that we did. But ... maybe it will make us even more restless because now we will be tied down in ways that we can no longer leave or change.

I found it difficult to offer much to them by way of advice. I sensed their restlessness; indeed, I often feel just that kind of dis-ease within my own life. My life is going on, full of many things, and, too often, I am absent from those things, too restless to receive the spirit of my own life. Rich life, life-giving love, true community, and God are present...but I, like the young couple I just talked about, am absent! Perhaps it sounds strange to suggest that we can be absent from our own lives, but, in fact, it is rare that we are present to what's taking place within our lives.

St. Augustine, in a famous prayer after his conversion, expresses this well:

> Late have I loved you, O Beauty ever ancient, ever new, late have I loved! *You were within me, but I was outside*, and it was there that I searched for you. In my unloveliness I plunged into the lovely things which you created. You *were with me, but I was not with you.* (*Confessions*, Book 7)

"You were within me, but I was outside." Few phrases more accurately describe how we relate to God, life, love, and community than does that line from Augustine. It is why my friends could have so rich a life and yet be so deeply restless; it is why we all generally look everywhere else rather than to our own lives for love and delight; and it is why we are perennially so deeply restless.

This restlessness cannot be stilled by a journey outward. It is inward that we need to go. Inside our own, actual lives, beyond our restless yearnings and fantasies, God, love, community, meaning, timeless significance, and everything else that we search for, are already there. We become bigger than our seemingly too small lives, not by finding and doing something extraordinary and timeless — great achievements, world fame, leaving a mark in history, being known by and connected to more and more people — but in being present to what is timeless and extraordinary within our ordinary lives.

I have a series of axioms that I try to meditate on regularly to keep myself aware of how, perennially, what I am yearning for is inside of me, but I am outside. Allow me to share them with you:

- *Life is what happens to you while you are planning your life.*

- *I always resented interruptions to my work until I realized that those interruptions were my real work.*

- *Who is my neighbor? My neighbor is the person who is actually in my life while I am plotting how to be in somebody else's life.*

- *Love is what you are experiencing while you are futilely searching for it beyond your own circles — and taking the circles around you for granted.*

- *Joy is what catches you by surprise, from a source that is quite other than where you are pursuing it.*

The Prayer of St. Francis captures the same thing — and it is that kind of prayer we need most when our restless yearning overwhelms us and our lives feel too small for us.

MOURNING INCOMPLETENESS

There is a story in the Old Testament that both shocks and fascinates by its sheer earthiness.

A certain king, Jephthah, is at war, and things are going badly for him and his army. In desperation he prays to God, promising that if he is granted victory he will, upon returning home, offer in sacrifice the first person he meets. His prayer is heard and he is given victory. When he returns home he is horrified because the first person he meets, whom he must now kill in sacrifice, is his only daughter, in the full bloom of her youth, whom he loves most dearly. He tells his daughter of his promise and offers to break it rather than sacrifice her. She, however, insists that he go through with his promise, but there is one condition: she needs, before she dies, time in the desert to bewail the fact that she is to die a virgin, incomplete, unconsummated. She asks her father for two months, during which she goes into the desert with her maiden companions and mourns her unfulfilled life. Afterward, she returns and offers herself in sacrifice (Judges 11).

Despite the patriarchal character of this story, it is a parable that in its own earthy way says something quite profound, namely, that we must mourn what is incomplete and unconsummated in our lives.

Karl Rahner once wrote that "in the torment of the insufficiency of everything attainable we begin to realize that here, in this life, all symphonies remain unfinished." He is correct.

In the end, we all die, like Jephthah's daughter, as virgins, our lives incomplete, our deepest dreams and deepest yearnings largely frustrated, still looking for intimacy, never having had the finished consummate symphony, unconsciously bewailing our virginity. This is true of married people just as it is true for celibates. Ultimately, we all sleep alone.

This must be mourned. Whatever form this might take, each of us must, at some point, go into the desert and bewail our virginity — mourn the fact that we will die unfulfilled, incomplete. It is when we fail to do this — and because we fail to do it — that we go through life being too demanding, too angry, too bitter, too disappointed, and too prone to blame others and life itself for our frustrations. When we fail to mourn properly our incomplete lives, then this incompleteness becomes a haunting depression, an unyielding restlessness, and a bitter center which robs our lives of all delight.

It is because we do not mourn our virginity that we demand that someone, or something — a marriage partner, a sexual partner, an ideal family, having children, an achievement, a vocational goal or job — take all our loneliness away. That, of course, is an unreal expectation which invariably leads to bitterness and disappointment.

In this life, there is no finished symphony. We are built for the infinite. Our hearts, minds, and souls are abysses, canyons without a bottom. Because of that, we will, this side of eternity, always be lonely, restless, incomplete, still a virgin — living in the torment of the insufficiency of everything attainable. My parents' generation tended to recognize this more easily than we do. They prayed, daily, the prayer: "To thee do we send up our sighs, mourning and weeping in this valley of tears." That prayer and others like it were their way of bewailing their virginity. Contemporary spirituality tends to reject as unhealthy and a bit morbid such an emphasis on the limitations of this life. That is arguable. What is not is the fact that we never, here in this life, get the full symphony, the panacea to our loneliness. Any balanced, truly life-giving spirituality must take this into account and challenge people to understand, integrate, and live out that fact.

Perhaps the best way to do this is not the way of my parents' generation, who sometimes put more emphasis on life after death than upon life after birth. Maybe it is a bit morbid to consider this life so much a "vale of tears." But tears must be taken into account. Otherwise, in the end, we are falsely challenged and the symbolic infrastructure of our spirituality is inadequate to handle our actual experience.

The daydreams of our childhood eventually die, but the source that ultimately fires them, our infinite caverns of feeling, do not. We ache just as much, even after we know the daydream can never, this side of eternity, come true. Hence, like Jephthah's daughter, there comes a time when we must go into the desert and mourn the fact that we are to die a virgin.

THE INWARD JOURNEY

In the preface to Elizabeth O'Connor's book *Search for Silence,* N. Gordon Cosby writes: "The one journey that ultimately matters is the journey into the place of stillness deep within one's self. To reach that place is to be at home; to fail to reach it is to be forever restless."

That's a scary thought, especially for those of us who are restless and who find it difficult to be comfortable alone and with silence. Yet there is no doubt that Cosby is right; not to reach inner stillness is to be forever restless. So it is good to make our peace with this. The journey inward, to that quiet center, that central silence, where one's own life and spirit are united with the life and Spirit of God, is long and arduous. Moreover, very little invites us to make it.

First of all, we are born restless, overcharged for our own lives, so on fire with eros and energy of every kind that simply sitting still is already itself a considerable task. This restlessness, which is the heartbeat of a human soul, is the fire of God within us and is God's assurance, written into nature, that we will not settle for anything less than everything. As Augustine so aptly put it: "You have made us for yourself, Lord, and our hearts are restless until they rest on you." Still, given all this, spontaneously our restlessness pushes us outward rather than inward. When we are restless, almost invariably, there is the compulsive desire to seek rest in something or somebody outside ourselves. Rarely, when we are deeply restless, are we drawn inward, to seek a solution to our yearnings in stillness and silence.

Almost everything within our world militates against journeying inward toward stillness and silence as a remedy to the painful obsessions that we experience in our restlessness. The world both intensifies and trivializes our restlessness. Our culture invites excitement, not silence; activity, not stillness. Thus we find ourselves constantly titillated and overstimulated in our restlessness. Somehow the impression is out there that everyone in the whole world is finding something that you are not, that everyone's life is more full and complete than yours, that your life, as it is, is too small and timid, and that only if you bring many more people, things, places, and experiences into your life will you find peace and calm. The world suggests that the solution to your restlessness lies outside yourself, in building a bigger and more exciting life. If you are lonely, find a friend; if you are restless, do something; if you have a desire, fulfill it!

The world also trivializes our restlessness, inviting us in a thousand ways to forget that God has called us to make an inward pilgrimage. The world, while not necessarily against God, invites us to forget God. "Distract yourself," it says. "Lower your ideals. Forget about immortal longings and eternal peace and think of your immediate frustrations, your lack of self-expression, your yearning hormones, and of how little of the good life you've actually got. Do more things, change marriage partners, make a career change, have a better sex life, travel more, read more books, go to more movies — or write a book, plant a tree, have a child! Find enough life and leave some mark and you won't be so restless!"

Given all of this, it is not easy for us to believe that the

ultimate solution to our restlessness lies in a journey inward.
Given all of this too, it is not easy to have the courage to
make that journey, even when we know that it must be done.
Cosby's challenge — "The one journey that ultimately matters is the journey into the place of stillness deep within one's
self. To reach that place is to be at home; to fail to reach it
is to be forever restless" — should be written in bold letters
in the preface of every spiritual book today. Too much inside of us and around us invites us to forget this, and it is
too dangerous to forget it. It is our rest, our peace, that is at
stake here.

When Christ invites us to make the preferential option for
the poor, he also spells out the consequence of ignoring the
invitation, namely, at the last judgment the king might not
recognize us since he never met us in the least of our broth-
ers and sisters. The invitation to move inward, in silence,
to gently calm our raging restlessness with an inner stillness
that comes from union with God is just as nonnegotiable. To
ignore it is to take a bad risk.

YOUNG IN GOD'S EYES

Several years ago, I spent two months living in the guest
house of a Trappist monastery. Visitors from many parts of
the world would pass through, spend a few days, have meals
together at a common table, and pass on.

One day an elderly couple passed through. They had retired twenty years earlier, traveled the earth, and seen many
of the world's greatest sights. They were describing all of this
when someone asked them: "Of all the things you've seen on
earth what was the most impressive?"

The husband answered: "This will sound strange, but it's
true! Of all the things we've seen, what impressed me the

most was the stones on the bottom of the Grand Canyon. They're only stones! But, as we were standing on the floor of the Grand Canyon, I was reading the tourist brochure and it said: 'The stones you are standing on are two billion years old.' Two billion years! When I think of my life in relationship to that, it isn't even as long as a snap of my fingers. I believe in eternal life, and so two billion years from now we are all going to still be alive. Putting life against that background kind of puts us into perspective now, doesn't it?"

It certainly does, and how badly we need that! The pains, tensions, and preoccupations of daily life habitually pin us obsessively into the here and now, making it almost impossible to think of life beyond our present problems and concerns. Our hearts, bodies, and heads ache, and the pressures and tensions of our lives simply overwhelm us and we cannot see beyond them. We spend most of our lives pathologically obsessed with our heartaches and headaches and, because of that, chronically depressed.

Using an analogy, this might be understood as follows: a young child breaks her favorite toy; she's disconsolate. Her mother tries to console her and reassures her that this was only a toy, that she soon will completely forget about it, and, years later, will joke about this incident and find it amusing. That is easy for the mother to say. She has lived long enough to know that time heals, opens up new perspectives, and colors the past in altogether new ways. She knows that life is long, that we outgrow the toys and obsessions of our childhood. From her perspective as an adult she can see how insignificant and transient is this particular experience of loss. But it is not so easy for the child. In her young mind and heart there is nothing to give perspective beyond the present loss and desolation. She sincerely believes that she will never be happy again, that nothing can heal this hurt.

As we grow from childhood to adulthood, gradually our perspective widens and, from that vantage point, we can look back with calm and amusement on many of the losses and hurts of our childhood (at least at broken toys). Within the perspective of a long life, they can appear as incidental, growing pains, amusing.

However, even as we see our childhood losses in this light, the tensions and obsessions of the present moment (fractured relationships, lost innocence, lost youth, lost health, lost limbs, lost jobs, lost honeymoons, lost families, and so on) make us just as disconsolate and narrowly depressed as did the broken toys of our childhood. When we suffer loss, we still believe in all sincerity that nothing will ever really make us happy again.

When this happens, it is hard for God, the great Mother, to console us and to assure us that, within the larger perspective, these heartaches and headaches too will pass and too will be eclipsed by perspectives beyond our present imagination and experience. When we ache inconsolably, it is hard to get through a given day or night — let alone think two billion years down the line! Yet to keep perspective, to keep our hurts from crushing us and our achievements from inflating us, and to keep ourselves from being old and despairing when we are still young and have eternal possibilities, we need to see our lives against this larger horizon. In terms of real life, in God's eyes, we are all still in eschatological diapers, irrespective of age! We are children, babies really, crying over broken toys.

This is also true with respect to our moral failures. We are children bumbling selfishly through life, needing to be challenged daily to share our toys with others. God, like any understanding parent, especially as one who has watched so many children grow up is, I am sure, doing more amused smiling at our smudged faces and dirty diapers than condemning.

When we live in depression or obsession we have lost perspective. We have forgotten how young we are, how understanding God is, and how old are the stones at the bottom of the Grand Canyon.

Chapter 2

Visible, Perceptible, Effective Proximities of God

Being Blessed into Life

A blessing is the visible, perceptible, effective proximity of God. A blessing demands to be passed on — it communicates itself to other people. To be blessed is to be oneself a blessing.

— DIETRICH BONHOEFFER

AN IRISH BLESSING...

May you have many friends
and may they be as mature
in taste and health and color
and as sought after
as the contents of this glass.

May you have warm words on a cold evening,
a full moon on a dark night,
and the road downhill all the way to your door.

May every hair on your head turn into a candle
to light your way to heaven.
And may God and his Holy Mother
take the harm of the years away from you.

And ... may you have no frost on your spuds,
no worms on your cabbage,
May your goat give plenty of milk,
and if you should buy a donkey
please, God, she be pregnant!

BLESSING AND CURSING LIFE

"And God saw that it was good, indeed it was very good!" This tells us how God feels about us and the world, and it contains the implication that we should feel the same way about ourselves and the rest of the world: "good, very good!"

This is the primary creational and anthropological affirmation within all of Scripture, and its challenge is as far-reaching as it is (when examined in the light of our actual lives) startling. To believe that we and our world are good, very good; to take delight in our lives and in each other; to live lives that radiate joy rather than depression, boredom, and resentment; well...that sounds simple and easy, but remains a rare thing that is seldom accomplished.

How many people do you know who take delight in their lives, in their families, in their spouses, in their friends? The rule is more depression. Rather than feeling delight and joy in our lives and our relationships we feel boredom, resentment, paranoia, jealousy, possessive clinging, or a sense of guilt or threat. "Delight" is rarely the word which describes what we feel about anything. Sadly, too, rather than helping create delight around us, we more commonly kill it. We tell our children to shut up and stop making so much noise when they are enthusiastic and full of life, and we generally feel the delight and laughter of others as a threat to our dullness and deadened sense of delight. Shouts of laughter, joy, and delight tend to irritate us, bringing a "will-you-shut-up" reaction rather than a calling to delight in the fact that "it is good, very good!"

After childhood, we rarely find it easy to delight in anything. Yet delight, along with gratitude, is the primary religious virtue and is the deepest root of all love, friendship, sexuality, family life, community, passion, and enthusiasm.

All of these, if they are not to die, must be a constant source of delight.

When delight is lost in love, friendship, sexuality, genitality, family life, community life, or our jobs and vocations, then depression, resentment, and self-pity take over and these soon enough tell love, friendship, sexuality, genitality, family, community, and creativity what we tell overenthusiastic children, namely, to "shut up"! When joy breaks down, eventually everything breaks down. When we stop blessing (which means precisely to affirm and delight in someone's joy, beauty, and creativity) we immediately begin to curse. To meet beauty, joy, laughter, and creativity with affirmation, to bask in them, to delight in them, is to bless. Any other response is a curse that brings death and is, in the truest meaning of that word, necrophilia: preferring to love what is dead rather than what is alive!

Why do we do that? Why, when our deepest desires are for delight and joy, do we constantly kill them within ourselves and within others? A simplistic line of argument suggests that the whole root of this lies in a distorted image of God. Simply put, this argument says that our past religious training injected into us the notion of an angry, defensive, anti-erotic, anti-enjoyment god who is threatened and angry when we are happy and experience pleasure so that every time we thoroughly enjoy something we feel like we are stealing pleasure from God.

There is some truth in that, though not nearly as much as many think. Given that the propensity to curse delight rather than bless it is as strong (or stronger) in persons who have journeyed far from the influence of the distorted religious training just mentioned, one suspects that the real culprit is more psychological than religious, namely, wounded narcissism.

We curse joy rather than bless it because we have been cursed rather than blessed whenever we manifested it (especially when we were very young). We do not take delight in ourselves and the world and we don't feel like they are "good and very good" because too few persons ever took delight in us and too few persons ever told us that we were "good and very good!" We tell overenthusiastic children to "shut up" because, when we were overenthusiastic children, we were told to "shut up"!

The most important challenge that all of us face in life, religiously and psychologically, is to overcome this and to bless rather than to curse. When we look at a child in a high-chair joyously smudging her face with food, when we hear the overenthusiastic noise of children shouting, and whenever we feel (in love, friendship, sexuality, community, or creativity) the power, beauty, and pleasure of life, we must respond with delight, saying: "God, it's good, it's so good!" Then, and only then, are we honoring our Creator, honoring ourselves, and moving beyond necrophilia to make love to what is truly alive.

RECEIVING A BLESSING

Several years ago, I preached a sermon on the baptism of Christ within which I remarked that the words that God speaks over Jesus at his baptism — "This is my beloved child in whom I take delight" — are words that God, daily, speaks over us. Some hours later my doorbell rang and I was approached by a young man who had heard my sermon and who was both moved and distraught by it.

He had not been to church for some time but had gone on this particular Sunday because he had, just that week, pleaded guilty to a crime and was awaiting sentence. He was soon to go to prison. The sermon had struck a painful chord inside him because, first of all, he had trouble believing that God, or anyone else, loved him; yet he wanted to believe it. Secondly, and even more painful, he believed that nobody had ever been pleased or delighted with him: "Father, I know that in my whole life nobody has ever been pleased with me. I was never good enough! Nobody has ever taken delight in anything I've ever done!" This man had never been blessed. Small wonder he was about to go to prison.

What does it mean to be blessed? What is a blessing?

The word "blessing" takes its root in the Latin verb *bene-dicere*, to speak well of (*bene* well, *dicere* to speak). Therefore to bless someone is to speak well of him or her. But this implies a special form of "speaking well." To bless someone is, through some word, gesture, or ritual, to make that person aware of three things: (1) the goodness of the original creation where, after making the earth and humans, God said that it was "good, very good"; (2) that God experiences the same delight and pleasure in him or her that God experienced with Jesus at his baptism when he said: "This is my beloved child in whom I take delight"; and (3) that we, who are giving the blessing, recognize that goodness and take that delight in the other person.

Thus, the ritual blessing that we are given at the end of a eucharist — "I bless you in the name of the Father, the Son, and the Holy Spirit" — could be paraphrased to sound like this: "As we leave this celebration, let us feel deeply and take with us the deep truth that we, the world, and our lives are good, very good. There is no need to live in guilt and depression. We are, despite our faults, very good and delightful to God. Let us, therefore, take delight in each other and in ourselves. We are, after all, extremely pleasing to God."

When I left home as a seventeen-year-old boy, my father and mother blessed me. They made me kneel on the old linoleum floor of our kitchen, placed their hands on my head, and said the ritual words of Christian blessing. In effect, however, what they were saying to me was: "We love you, we trust you, we are proud of you, and we send you off with our full spirit. You are our beloved child, and in you we are well pleased." I suspect that had the young man I spoke of above been blessed in the same way by his parents, or by anyone else significant to him, he would not have been on his way to prison. To be unblessed is to be bleeding in a very deep place.

So much of our hunger is a hunger for blessing. So much of our aching is the ache to be blessed. So much of our sadness comes from the fact that nobody has ever taken delight and pleasure in us in a nonexploitive way. When has anyone ever made you the object of delight? When has anyone taken, in a nonexploitive way, delight in your body, your beauty, your intelligence, your person? When have you last felt that you are someone in whom others, and God, take pleasure and delight?

Only a few, I suspect, move about in their daily lives with the joy, confidence, and grace that comes from knowing that they are, as persons, good, beautiful, and objects of delight. Depression is more the rule. Most of us are more like the young man spoken of above — bleeding, less than whole, unconfident, depressed, going through life without a sense either of its goodness or of our own, going through life without being able to really give or experience delight.

Scripture says that when Jesus was baptized the spirit came to him in *bodily form* and said: "This is my beloved child; in him I take delight!" What we need, more than anything else, is to give bodily form to this blessing. We need, daily, within our families and within our relationships in general, to do things and say things that help those around us believe that life is good, that their lives are good, that they are good, and that we, and God, look on them with great pleasure and delight.

BLESSING AS SEEING

To really see someone, especially someone who looks up to you, is to give that person an important blessing. In a gaze of recognition, of understanding, in an appreciative look, there is deep blessing. Often it is not important that we say much to those for whom we are significant, but it is very important that we see them.

A couple of years ago, a family that I know had a painful incident with their thirteen-year-old daughter. She was caught shoplifting. As things turned out, she was stealing things that she neither needed or wanted. Moreover, in her case, her stealing these things was not, as it often is among teens, something intended to impress peers, a little rite of passage necessary for acceptance into a group of friends. No, without her saying so, she was stealing to get her father's attention. Her father, struggling in his relationship with her mother, was not around a great deal and did not give a lot of attention to his daughter. So she forced his hand. It was he that she demanded come to the police station to pick her up and settle things with the police. In doing that he had to give his daughter his attention. He had to look at her. Her shoplifting was a way of forcing her father to see her.

There is a deep longing inside us to be seen by those to whom we look up — our parents, our elders, our leaders, our teachers, our coaches, our pastors, and our bosses. It is important to us, more than we generally imagine, that those who are above us look at us, see us, recognize us.

We see this acted out ritually, for instance, when someone has an audience with the pope. In such an audience, not many words are exchanged. The idea is not so much to have a deep conversation with the pope as it is to be seen by him. It is important that the pope *sees* you, that he recognizes you, that his appreciative gaze falls upon you. There is a certain blessing imparted in that and, contemporary cynicism notwithstanding, those who have had an audience with the pope, or with the queen or some royalty, have some feeling for what this is. Blessing by seeing is one of the deep archetypal functions of all royalty, of all parents, and of all who lead others in any way.

Good kings and queens see their people; good parents see their kids; good teachers see their students; good pastors see their parishioners; good coaches see their players; good executives see their employees; and in really good restaurants the owner comes round to the tables and sees his or her customers, and the customers are, without being able to explain why, grateful that the owner took the time and pain to see them. We are blessed by being seen.

At a primal level we see this need to be blessed by being seen acted out in every playground on earth. The little child is playing at something but constantly looking about for the parent and saying: "Mummy, watch me!" "Daddy, watch me!" And more than one is the mother who cannot get any work done because her toddler is demanding every minute that mummy look at her or him.

My point is that today the young are not being seen enough in this way. Our youth, much like the thirteen-year-old girl referred to earlier, are acting out in all kinds of ways as a means of getting our attention. They want to, and they *need* to, be seen by us — parents, adults, teachers, priests, leaders. They need our blessing. They need to see, right in our eyes, the radical acceptance of their reality, and they need to read in our eyes the words: "You are my beloved child; in you I am well pleased." Youth need our appreciative gaze; mostly they simply need our gaze. One of the deepest hungers inside young people is the hunger for adult connection, the desire to be recognized, seen, by a significant adult.

The surface often belies this. We can easily be fooled and put off here. Our young people will, precisely, tend to give us the impression that they neither want nor need us, that we should go away and leave them to their own world. Nothing could be further from the truth. They desperately need, and badly want, the blessing that comes from our gaze and presence. They need us to see them. In the end, more than they want our words, they want our gaze. And so much of their acting out, the shoplifting, the drugs, the insolence, and the absence, are little more than an attempt to force our hand, to demand and beg: "Mummy, Daddy, someone significant and adult, watch me!'

BLESSING AS DYING TO GIVE LIFE

We all live with constricted hearts. There is a tightness, an unfreedom, a timidity, a tangle of constrictions, inside each of us that blocks warmth and intimacy. We try things to get at it, to dissolve it, to free ourselves. So it is no accident that we are so obsessed with therapy, sex, achievement, intellectual and artistic pursuit, and quick solace in religion. We are trying to free our hearts. Sadly, for the most part, we are not succeeding all that well because the heart is not set free by the intellect, the groin, nor even the hands. It is set free through blessing. Blessing deconstricts the heart.

Blessing has various components: to bless others is, first of all, to see them, to genuinely see them, to look at them so that they sense that they are truly being recognized. Then, and this need not always be put into words but can be present right in that seeing, to bless others is to take delight in them, to give them the gaze of admiration, to look at them in a way that says: "You are my beloved child; in you I take delight!" But that is not all. If I want to really bless someone, I must, in some way, give my life to that person so as to enable him or her to have more life. To really bless someone is to, in some way, die for that person.

We see this powerfully portrayed in Victor Hugo's classic *Les Miserables* (both in the book and in the recent musical production). At one point in that story, Jean Val Jean, who is by then an old man, goes in search of Marius, the young man who is in love with his adopted daughter. Initially his motivation for searching out Marius is mixed. He wants to see who this young man is, what he looks like, and form an opinion of him. He is also, at this stage, understandably threatened by this young man who is, after all, taking his daughter away from him. So he goes in search of him.

He, Jean Val Jean, finds him at the barricades, with a group of idealistic young revolutionaries who, while trying to help the poor, have put themselves into a position where they are all about to be killed in a brutal attack from government forces. Their position is hopeless. The almost certain possibility is that, tomorrow, when that attack comes, they will all die, including Marius. Jean Val Jean senses their idealism, but he also senses, beneath their bravado, a lot of fear. For all their idealism and courage, they are, underneath it all, still frightened boys.

It is in this situation that he finds young Marius, asleep. Jean Val Jean bends over him and says a prayer of blessing. He begins by invoking God ("God on high, hear my prayer . . . "), and then, turning to young Marius, he continues speaking to God, repeating several times: "Look on this boy . . . he is young, he's afraid...tomorrow he might die, but, Lord, let him live — let me die; let him live! Let him live!"

Those last lines are the prototype of deep blessing. They explain too why blessings work from the top down — from God to us, from old to young, from empowered to disempowered, from those who have full life to those who have not. They also show what is demanded in a deep blessing, namely, a giving away of life, a dying so that someone else might now have life. A blessing is not just simply an affirmation: "You are a fine young man!" "You are a gifted young woman!" "I believe in you!" "I trust you!" These affirmations, good and life-giving as they are, are not enough. To bless someone deeply is to die for that person in some real way, to really die, to give up some real life for that person.

Good parents, good mothers and fathers, do that for their children. In all kinds of ways, they sacrifice their lives for their children. They die, but their children live. Good teachers do that for their students, good mentors do that for their protégés, good priests do that for their parishioners, good doctors and nurses do that for their patients, good politicians do that for their countries, and any good elder who truly blesses a young person does that for that young person.

Do you want to bless a young person? Give her your job! Give him some of your power. Step back and let her assume some of the leadership you have been exercising. Let his opinion overrule yours. Look at her and, like Jean Val Jean, pray to God: "Let me die! Let her live!"

PASSING ON A BLESSING

Several years ago, at a workshop in Los Angeles, John Shea shared a story that speaks of the effect of a deep blessing. It is the story of a woman whom he met while teaching in Ireland.

During a summer school there, he had asked the people in his class to recount an incident of blessing from their own lives, and one woman, very timidly, shared the following:

The incident took place when she was twelve years old, on a Sunday morning. She came from a large family, and each Sunday morning to get them ready for church her mother would line up all of her children and then, one by one, wash each child's face and comb each one's hair. Each would wait patiently in line for a turn and then go out to play while the mother finished the rest. One Sunday the woman telling the story was second in line and anxious to get her turn over with because it would mean nearly a half hour of play time while the others were being washed and combed. Then, just before her turn, her mother noticed that the youngest sister, at the end of the line, was missing a shoelace and asked her to go into the bedroom and get one. But, not wanting to lose her place in the line and given that her mother did not ask her a second time, she did not go. Her mother said nothing as she combed her hair. When she was finished she went out to play. However after playing for about ten minutes she felt guilty and went back into the house to get the shoelace for her baby sister. When she entered the house, the mother had just removed her own shoelace and was bent down, putting it into her baby sister's shoe. Feeling doubly guilty, she went into her parents' bedroom and got a shoelace and, as her mother was combing her baby sister's hair, she bent down and put the shoelace into her mother's shoe. While she was doing this, her mother said nothing but gently stroked her hair.

When she finished telling that story, somebody in the class asked her what it meant and, rather embarrassed, she said: "I don't know, but it has just stayed with me all these years!"

A day later, Shea, who during this two-week course had

the habit of sitting under a particular tree every day during the afternoon break and smoking a cigar, had settled himself under that tree, but had forgotten to bring a cigar. Out of nowhere, the woman appeared: "Where is your cigar today?" she asked shyly. "I forgot to bring one!" he answered. Immediately she produced a cigar, gave it to him, and without a word disappeared. The next day after his conference, Shea found her sitting by herself at the back of the room. He went to her and confronted her with these words: "The cigar is the shoelace, isn't it?" "Yes," she answered, "ever since that day that my mother stroked my hair, through all these years, and long after she has died, I have had this secret covenant with her, I go through life supplying what is missing!" Blessing begets blessing. When we are treated gently, gentleness grows in us. We all make an unconscious secret covenant with those who have blessed us, who have stroked our hair gently.

Listening to Shea's story, I was reminded of the words of Li-Young Lee, the fine Chinese American poet, who recounts a similar incident with his own father. In a poem entitled, "The Gift," he recounts how, when he was a boy of seven, his father recited a story to him to help calm the pain as he removed a metal splinter from his son's hand. He cannot remember any longer the story his father told that day, but he can remember his father's tenderness, his gentle voice, and how it soothed the fear and the pain of a seven-year-old who was frightened of dying from a splinter: "Had you entered that afternoon, you would have thought you saw a man planting something in a boy's palm, a silver tear, a tiny flame."

Now, no longer a boy, the poet is taking a splinter out of his wife's hand, and what his father put in his hand that afternoon all those years ago is now inside him:

Look how I shave her thumbnail down so carefully she feels no pain. Watch as I lift the splinter out. I was seven when my father took my hand like this, and I did not hold that shard between my fingers and think, *metal that will bury me,* christen it Little Assassin, Ore Going Deep for my Heart. And I did not lift up my wound and cry, *Death visited here!* I did what a child does when he's given something to keep. I kissed my father.

When we bless others, stroking them gently with understanding and forgiveness, we make secret covenants, giving them something to keep.

DECONSTRICTING THE HEART

We long for love, to share our hearts, minds, and bodies with others. It is easier with the head and with the body; we are less adept at sharing our hearts.

Invariably, even within our most intimate relationships, it is the heart that holds back, tentative, tight, constricted, not fully able to open and reveal and release itself. In most intimate relationships this is the frequent complaint: "You only share ideas, you never reveal your heart!" "We have sex, but our souls never meet!" "Your heart is not really in this, even though you claim it is!"

Confronted with this, the temptation of our own age is to look for an answer in sex. Our age would have us believe that the way to deconstrict the heart is through sex. The complex human heart, with all its blockages, tightness, chasms, and constrictions, to today's mind is set free by sex. Small wonder that sex is paraded as salvation, used to sell virtually every product, and becomes the make-it-or-break-it item in so many relationships. We see it as the key to intimacy.

But sex does not automatically, nor easily, insure intimacy because the release of the heart has less to do with sex than it has to do with blessing. Among many mammals, the mother deconstricts the baby after it is born by licking its entire body, thus stripping off the membranes which in the womb had helped cradle, protect, and feed that new life but which now bind and paralyze it. In doing this, the mother opens the newborn to life, sets it free to walk on its own, to romp in the sun. In the mammal world, this is primary blessing — the mother setting her young free, the elder giving the young their birthright.

Now imagine a man and woman standing before each other, able to relate to each other sexually and intellectually, to share both their bodies and their minds, but one (or both) of them frustrated because the other's heart is not open and is not a part of the relationship in the same way as is that other's body and mind. What is needed in this relationship is not more sex, but a blessing (which oftentimes the couple cannot give to each other). The tightness in the heart that is making it more tentative than the body and the head has often less to do with that particular relationship than it has to do with lack of blessing from "elders" in the other areas of life.

The heart is set free by blessing from our "elders." This is symbolized primarily by the mother licking the afterbirth off of her young. It is made whole when somebody who is our "elder" affirms us, somebody who is our "elder" because something about them — they gave us birth, their superior age, or wisdom, or virtue, or talent, or position — puts them into a position where we need them to set us free, where we are dependent upon them in such a way that their affirmation or curse either binds or looses us. They, figuratively and really, have power to lick us free of constricting afterbirth or to leave us thus paralyzed.

What all this means is that the cure for the man who stands before his wife unable to relate to her with his heart as he does with his head and his body has less to do with his sexual and intellectual relationship to her than it has to do with lack of blessing elsewhere in his life. If his father would one day affirm him in his marriage and in his work, if his mother would one day make it clear to him that he should feel free from all her expectations, if his boss at work would one day call him in and tell him that his work is valuable — well, that night his wife, whose constant complaint is that he never talks about his feelings, would find that she would not be able to shut him up. His heart would be bubbling over and she would suddenly notice a vital new dimension, the heart, in their relationship.

The same holds true in reverse. If a woman were one day to receive the unconditional affirmation of her father or mother and then, on that same day, be made aware by the dean of her department that her work is valuable and he does not perceive this as a threat but as a joy to be shared, she would find her heart suddenly and joyfully deconstricted and her lucky husband wouldn't know what hit him. The way to deconstrict the heart is more through blessing than through sex. Once we know this, we might be more understanding of each other, and we might as we get older look more for a younger person to bless than for a younger person to sleep with.

BLESSED BY OUR ROOTS

Several years ago when I still taught on a college staff, I had a colleague, a priest, who used to travel nearly two hundred miles regularly to visit his invalid mother. She was ninety years old, almost totally incapacitated, couldn't recognize her son, couldn't speak to him or make any form of rational contact. Yet her son would visit her regularly, just to sit quietly at her bedside. For him, there was no rational contact, but there was tremendously meaningful contact: "I go and sit by my mother's bed and it steadies me, it centers me in some deep inchoate way. I always leave after a visit with a much surer sense of who I am and what I believe in. After sitting with my mother, for a while at least, I know who I am!"

I experienced something quite similar recently when our extended family gathered for a family reunion. On my father's side we are a large clan, and when we gather for a full reunion every ten years, almost three hundred people show up. But it is not just the chance to see long lost relatives that makes this a special gathering. For most of us, almost as important as the people is the place. We meet for a weekend at our old parish grounds in a very remote farming region where our grandfather and grandmother and some of their friends and relatives came and homesteaded nearly a hundred years ago — and where most of us grew up. Our grandparents were the first persons ever to break the soil there, to build houses there, to raise families there, and to build a church there. That church still stands, a very humble stone and cement building, alone among some lonely hills. It is still used for worship by the local parish, which consists mainly of relatives. My parents are buried in the church cemetery.

Something happens when we gather there that goes far beyond the simple nostalgia of seeing the old place, reminiscing with relatives you haven't seen for ten years, and visiting your parents' graves. There is a deep experience of coming *home*, of sitting by the bedside of a silent mother who, while she cannot talk to you, can steady you and help you sort out who you are and what you really believe in. To touch your roots is to be nurtured by them, to drink strength from them, and to be steadied and given solid direction from the trunk that they have produced. Like my priest friend's experience with his aged mother, there isn't rational communication, but there is mystical touch, a dusting off and a branding of what lies deepest in the mind and heart. We know most truly who we are when we are at home.

Anthropologists today tell us that home is as much about place as it is about kinship, blood relationship, and family or psychological bonding. To be at home, one needs a place, a *homeland*.

Sadly today, for many of us, there is no longer any sense of home as place, no homeland. In a world of transience, of future shock — when people, organizations, knowledge, things, and places move through our lives at an ever increasing rate — where perhaps we have never been able to sink meaningful roots in any one place, it is no accident that more and more of us find ourselves morally lonely and anything but steady. Instability, confusion, and a deep moral loneliness are born of transience. When we have no place to identify with, no roots to drink from, no tree trunk to give us clear direction, it is no accident that we can on any given day sincerely wonder who we really are, what our values are, what we mean, and which of our seeming multiple personalities is our true one. From lack of home we suffer schizophrenia, dislocation, and much loneliness, both psychologically and morally. And part of that lack of home has to do with place. Place is also a home, a mother, we need to go back to occasionally.

It is no accident that land can be considered holy and that so many wars have been fought over the Holy Land, that aboriginal peoples feel so utterly dislocated once they have lost their lands, and that living in exile, away from one's homeland, for anyone, is so painful and disorienting. These things have to do with the loss of home, and home, in this case, means place.

Our old church back home stands on a hill, itself surrounded by miles and miles of desolate prairie hills. Those
lonely hills are silent. I looked at them long and hard a few
weeks ago, standing with some of my family by the graves
of my mother and father. We said some prayers, and we felt
from our deceased parents and from those silent lonely hills
a strength, a joy, and a steadiness that, for that time at least,
took away a lot of moral loneliness.

Chapter 3

The Torment of the Insufficiency of Everything Attainable

Loneliness, Longing, and Sexuality

There's a loneliness that can be rocked. Arms crossed, knees drawn up; holding, holding on, this motion, unlike a ship's, smooths and contains the rocker. It's an inside kind — wrapped tight like skin. Then there is a loneliness that roams. No rocking can hold it down. It is alive, on its own. A dry and spreading thing that makes the sound of one's own feet seem to come from a far-off place.

— Toni Morrison, *Beloved*

I was at ease in everything to be sure, but at the same time satisfied with nothing. Each joy made me desire another. I went from festivity to festivity. On occasion I danced for nights on end, ever madder about people and life. At times, late on those nights when dancing, the slight intoxication, my wild enthusiasm, everyone's violent unrestraint would fill me with a tired and overwhelmed rapture, it would seem to me — that at last I understood the secret of creatures of the world. But my fatigue would disappear the next day, and with it the secret.... Because I longed for eternal life, I went to bed with harlots and drank for nights on end. — Albert Camus, *The Fall*

MORAL LONELINESS

Some years ago, I wrote a book within which I suggested that there are *four* basic kinds of human loneliness: *alienation, restlessness, rootlessness,* and *psychological depression.* Were I to write such a book today, I would add another kind, *moral loneliness.*

49

As human beings, we are born with deep and multifarious longings. There is a fire inside of us that aches insatiably. At every level, body, psyche, soul, we feel our unwholeness and are restlessly driven to seek consummation with others and the world beyond us. We never quite overcome this in this life, but are always alone, restless, rootless, and depressed. Like Adam before the creation of Eve, we survey what is around us and long for something that will take away our aloneness. This constitutes the fundamental disease of the human person. Sometimes this longing is more inchoate and we are not clear what precisely we are lonely for. At other times our aching is very focused and we are so obsessed with a certain person that we lose all emotional freedom. Sometimes we are lonely in both ways, inchoately and compulsively, but always we are lonely.

When we examine loneliness within our current culture, it is all too easy to conclude that, ultimately, we are lonely for sexual union. For reasons too complex to examine here, our culture has tied the final solution for loneliness to romantic sexuality. This is so true that today the very expression "lover" connotes a sexual partner. In our culture the common impression is that we will be lonely until we have the right romantic sexual partner, and as a corollary it follows that the right sexual partner will be a panacea for our loneliness.

There is some truth in all of that, despite its one-sidedness. Sexual union in its truer forms is indeed the "one-flesh" consummation decreed by the Creator after the condemnation of loneliness: "It is not good for man to be alone." Outside sexual union one is in the end always somewhat alone, single, separate, cut off, a minority of one.

However, sexual union itself, as the history of human sexual experience reveals, is no guarantee of a consummation that alleviates aloneness. Ultimately, we are lonely at levels that sex alone cannot get at. Our deepest aloneness is moral. Where we feel most alone is, precisely, in the deepest part of our being, our moral soul, the place where we feel most strongly about the right and wrong of things and where what is most precious to us is cherished, guarded, and feels violated when it is attacked. Not often does anyone penetrate that dwelling. Why? Because where what is most precious lies is also where we are the most vulnerable to violation. We are, and rightly so, deeply cautious about whom we admit to the room wherein lives what is most precious.

Most often in that house we are alone. A fierce loneliness results, a moral loneliness. More deeply than we long for a sexual partner, we long for moral affinity, for someone to visit us in that deep part of us where all that is most precious to us is cherished and guarded. Our deepest longing is for a partner to sleep with morally, a kindred spirit, a soul mate in the truest meaning of that phrase.

Great friendships and great marriages invariably have this deep moral affinity at their root. The persons in these relationships are "lovers" in the true sense because they sleep with each other at that deep level, irrespective of whether or not there is sexual union. At the level of feeling, this type of love is experienced as a certain "coming home." Sometimes it is surrounded by romantic feelings and sexual attraction. Always, though, there is the sense that the other is a kindred spirit whose affinity with you is founded upon valuing most preciously what you value most preciously. You feel less alone because, in that place where you cherish and guard all that is most precious to you, you know that you are no longer a minority of one. Like Adam looking at Eve, you have now found someone of whom you can truly say: "At last, flesh of my flesh, bone of my bone!"

Therese of Lisieux suggests that as humans we are "exiles of the heart" and we must overcome this through mysticism, that is, precisely by moral communion with each other through sleeping with each other in charity, joy, peace, patience, goodness, long-suffering, faith, fidelity, mildness, and chastity. A culture which does not value sufficiently non-genital love because it is considered "just platonic" might well examine what it means to be morally lonely and what, in our loneliness, we are really looking for.

AN OPEN LETTER
FROM A RESTLESS PILGRIM

Recently I received a letter from a lady whom I have never met, but who occasionally writes to me. She writes when she is frustrated, and unable to talk to those she knows. I have a number of such letters from her and, despite different dates and wording, they all have roughly the same sound. Let me, with her permission, open up these letters for you. I synthesize and paraphrase:

Dear Father (Reader),
    I don't know why I am writing to you. We don't know each other, but I thought maybe we might understand each other. Allow me to introduce myself. My name is Karin, but that is not important, though you need to know some of my background to understand what I'm sharing.
    In fact, I don't quite know what I am sharing, but I am going to give this a try. I'll start with the feeling and then try to fill in some background. I'm frustrated and on the surface there should be no reason for this since I'm young (just turned forty), healthy, happily

married (in that I think I don't have enough reasons in my marriage to be unhappy), have two nearly grown (healthy and good) children, have a job that I basically like and that gives me some creative outlet, have some very supportive friends, and, while not rich, am also not poor. There's no one big thing that is radically weighing on me.

But that's the smooth surface. Some other things lurk underneath. They don't seem all that big or serious, but they can at times, like right now, render everything else pretty unsatisfying and make me almost hopelessly restless and frustrated.

The frustration I am talking about is not some big existential angst, like Camus and Bergman talk about, or even midlife crisis, or the types of things they suggest therapy for nowadays (victim of childhood abuse, adult child of an alcoholic, lack of self-esteem). I even did therapy once for some of those things (and it helped). But this is unconnected to that.

It's frustrating to talk about because it seems like such a small thing, something of no importance, certainly not something that should outweigh my blessings. But yet, it's there, and it doesn't go away. So I'm struggling and frustrated.

I want to share my person (my values and my spirit) in a way that I am not sharing them right now, especially in my marriage (but everywhere else too). Nobody seems interested, at least not most of the time. My husband is a good man, the proverbial "Israelite without guile," but he isn't interested in this kind of sharing or self-disclosure. He prefers an emotional and spiritual celibacy, even when he doesn't like sexual celibacy. With some of my other friends, there's depth to a point, but almost always there is a line that we don't cross. It seems there is always one block or another to this kind of sharing. It's the wrong time, or the wrong place, or the wrong people are around, or we're too tired, or the mood isn't right.

Sometimes I wonder who is interested in anything beyond the simple sweetening of life!

All this probably makes me sound like the typical person who is frustrated by the plainness of a life and a marriage which don't measure up to the ideals and expectations of romance and self-fulfillment in the culture. Maybe there's a bit of that here. But that's not my frustration. I am not naive about romance, nor about salvation lying in self-fulfillment. I'm old enough to have known another time (my parents' poverty, their making do, their sometimes crushing realism). That's in my genes. I grew up praying daily the words "to thee we send up our sighs, mourning and weeping in this valley of tears." If anything, I am a crushing realist. I am hardly looking for the finished symphony, the perfect consummation in a marriage or elsewhere, though I dream of it. I know enough of life (and romance and marriage) to know that in some fashion all of us will always sleep alone. What I'm looking for is not a lover, good sex, an affair with somebody who's sensitive and who will make everything better.

So what am I looking for? Maybe this letter is just trying to name it. A kindred spirit maybe? Somebody to sleep with in a different way? (But would that be an infidelity to my marriage?) Some ear to simply really hear me? Some other person to know what it's like? A statement of frustration that would overcome the torture of repressed expression? A saying out loud of a whispered truth that in this world we are all celibates whether we marry or not?

You tell me. Am I filling in what is lacking in the sufferings of Christ or am I just neurotic as hell? Is my marriage, such as it is, all I should expect or am I sell-ing myself short? Is my life, such as it is, all I should expect or am I being sold short? Am I suffering Christ's loneliness or am I just a frustrated woman approaching middle age? What's the difference between being a pil-grim on earth or just being sexually frustrated? What is proper expectation?

Please write to me and venture some opinion. Right now I don't know.

Peace,

Karin

CULTIVATING LONELINESS

Few persons in recent centuries have touched the human heart as deeply as Søren Kierkegaard, the Danish philosopher. He was a man of rare brilliance, with a lot to give others.

One of the reasons that he was able so deeply and excep-tionally to touch people's hearts, however, had less to do with this brilliance that it had to with his suffering, especially his loneliness.

Albert Camus once suggested that it is in solitude and loneliness that we find the threads that bind human commu-nity. Kierkegaard understood this, and he embraced it to the point that he positively cultivated his own loneliness. As a young man, he fell deeply in love and for a time planned mar-riage with the woman to whom he was passionately attached. However, at one stage, at great emotional cost to himself and (so history would suggest) at even a greater emotional cost to the woman involved, he broke off the engagement and set himself to live for the rest of his life as a celibate. His reasoning was simple. He felt that what he had to give to the world came a lot from his own loneliness. He could share deeply because, first of all, he felt deeply. Loneliness gave him depth. Rightly or wrongly, he judged that marriage might in some way deflect or distract him from that depth, painful as it was.

I suspect that there is a part of us that will smile at his reasoning. Marriage is hardly a panacea for loneliness! As well, a part of us will, no doubt, be critical of what seems to be implied in this, namely, that celibacy is somehow superior spiritually to being married.

However, there is a part in us too, that place where our mysticism resides, that, I submit, understands exactly what is at stake here. What Kierkegaard understood, not perfectly of course since this always remains partly inchoate for everyone, is the connection between loneliness and mysticism, longing and community.

What is meant by this? How do we connect to each other in and through our loneliness and longing? What does it mean that we are in mystical connection with each other?

Thomas Aquinas once suggested that there are two ways of being in union with something or with somebody: through actual possession or through desire. What is implied by the former of these notions is fairly clear. The latter needs explication. How are we in union with each other in and through desire? In his prize-winning novel *The Famished Road,* Ben Okri describes a Nigerian mother chiding her overly restless son for haunting her dreams: "Stay out of my dreams! That's not your place! I'm married to your father!" That's a most curious rebuke — scolding someone for being in your dreams! But the mystic within us understands this. In our restlessness and loneliness, just as in our prayers and blessings for each other, we haunt each other's dreams and each other's hearts in ways that are just as real as in any physical touch. By entering deeply into our own loneliness, we deeply enter each other's dreams.

Kierkegaard understood this and worried that if his marriage interfered with his loneliness it would interfere with his power to enter into our dreams. Partly this is mystical and is better accessed through feeling than through thought. Partly, though, this can be given expression: our loneliness is a privileged medium through which to enter our own hearts. Listening to our own loneliness puts us in touch with ourselves.

In our dreams we are also introduced to each other. In letting our loneliness haunt us, we begin, in the best sense of that phrase, to haunt each other's dreams. In loneliness and longing empathy is born. When nothing is foreign to us nobody will be foreign to us — and our words will begin to heal others.

"What is a poet?" Kierkegaard once asked. His answer: "A poet is an unhappy person who conceals deep torments in his or her heart, but whose lips are so formed that when a groan or shriek streams over them it sounds like beautiful music."

LOVE, LONELINESS, AND DISAPPOINTMENT

When we are young and hear longing and sadness in love songs, we think that the sadness and disappointment are a *prelude* to the experience of love and not really the result of its experience. Later, with a deeper experience, we realize that the sadness, longing, and disappointment ultimately originate not from the fact that love has not taken place, but that human love is finite. This insight helps us realize that the first task in any love, whether in a marriage or in a deep friendship, is for the two persons to console each other for the limits of their love, for the fact that they cannot not disappoint each other.

Why? Why can't two persons ever be enough for each other? Why is disappointment part of the experience of every marriage and friendship?

First of all, the very way that we are made precludes ever having, in this life, a oneness of mind, heart, and body that fulfills us in such a way that there is no disappointment. Our eros, our longing, is just too wide. We wake to life and consciousness with an abysmal longing. Our hearts, minds, and bodies are restless until they rest in God.

Thus, in this life (outside of rare and very transitory mystical experience) there is no consummation, sexual, emotional, psychological, or even spiritual with another person which is so deep and all-encompassing as to exclude all distance, shadow, and emptiness. No matter how deep a friendship or a marriage and no matter how good, rich in personality, and deep the other person may be, we always find ourselves somewhat disappointed. In this life, there is no union that fills every emptiness inside us.

Moreover, there is no union which fulfills perfectly the Genesis prescription that "two become one flesh." Disappointment in love arises not just because we are fired into life with an eros which only the infinite can fulfill. It also arises, and perhaps this causes the greater disappointment, because in the end in this life two can never ultimately become one.

No matter how deep a union in friendship or marriage, we always remain separate, two persons who cannot really ever, in this life, make just one heart, one mind, and one body.

No love or friendship ever fully takes away our separateness. Sometimes sexual electricity or emotional and spiritual affinity can, in their power, promise such a oneness. Sadly, in the end, they cannot fully deliver it. No matter how deep and powerful a union, ultimately we remain, and need to remain, in charge of our own hearts, minds, and bodies. This needs to be recognized, not just, as will be suggested later, to help us creatively deal with the disappointment, but especially so that we do not violate each other. What is implied here?

In this life we are always, to a degree, in exile from each other. In this sense we stand alone. Where we feel this most deeply is not in our sexual separation, but in our moral isolation. What we crave even more deeply than sexual unity is moral affinity, to be truly of one heart with another. More than we desire a lover, we desire a kindred spirit. If this is true, and I submit it is, then the deepest violations of each other are also not sexual (however deep and violent these may be) but moral. It's when we try to take charge of somebody else's soul (more so even than another's body) that we rape that person.

Finally, beyond even this, we are disappointed in love because in the end we are all to a degree limited, inadequate, blemished, dull, and boring. No matter how rich our personalities or attractive our bodies, none of us can indefinitely excite and generate novelty, sexual electricity, and psychological pleasure within a relationship. A relationship is like a long trip and, as Daniel Berrigan puts it, "there's bound to be some long dull stretches. Don't travel with someone who expects you to be exciting all the time!"

It is the recognition of the fact that, in love, we cannot not disappoint each other that makes it possible for us to remain in marriage, friendship, celibacy, and respect. It is when we demand not to be disappointed that we grow angry, make unrealistic demands, and violate each other's moral (and often sexual) integrity. Conversely, when we recognize the limits of love, when we accept an inevitable separateness, moral lone- liness, and disappointment, we will begin to console each other in our friendships and our marriages. In that consola- tion, since it touches so deeply our pilgrimed exiled status, we will begin to touch the threads that can bind us in a oneness of mind and heart beyond disappointment.

PASSION AND PURITY

Someone once said that the church does not understand pas- sion while the world does not understand purity. That might be rather simplistic and a dangerous generalization but, to my mind, it contains some important truth. Too often the church's concern for purity blocks it from properly appro- priating passion, just as the world's unbridled romance with passion generally blinds it to the importance of purity.

Clearly there are within the church individual voices and traditions, important ones, which cannot be accused of not understanding passion. However, that is not the general pic- ture. More commonly, at least in how the church is perceived by the world, there is the image of an institution that is so concerned for purity, especially sexual purity, that it fears passion and positively denigrates it. Many people, in fact, perceive the church as anti-erotic and anti-sexual, as an in- stitution that, regarding passion and sex, is excessively fearful, timid, paranoid, and restrictive. In the world, the church is seen as the enemy of passion.

That is a perception and perhaps it is unfair. People per- ceive things quite subjectively, and the church is often as much the scapegoat as it is villain. Moreover, some of the church's cautiousness with passion is not without legitimacy.

Passion without proper checks has led to an early grave for more than a few loves and lives. Still, in the end, the church has been, and still is, too fearful here. It doesn't understand passion.

On the other hand, the world does not understand purity. Purity and any type of chaste hesitancy is, in our world, regarded with a disapproval bordering on disdain. Purity is, for the most part, seen as naivete, as lack of nerve, as lack of drive for life. To believe in purity, especially sexual purity, is tantamount to believing in Santa and the Easter Bunny. Not all of this is bad; an excessive concern for purity can crush life, rob it of its earthiness, its spontaneity, and many of its deep pleasures. To love in real life is to stain the purity of our baptismal robes and our childhood dreams. Living and loving are messy businesses, and to be excessively given over to purity is to be a prude. Our world, in fact, does the church a huge favor when it points this out. Beyond this, however, the world does itself immeasurable harm by not understanding the place of purity and chastity. More emotional chaos, heartbreak, hardness of heart, and raging restlessness result from this lack of understanding than our world would ever have the courage to admit. To lose purity and chastity is to lose innocence. To lose innocence is to lose happiness. Our eyes may be opened but we are walking steadily out of the garden of paradise.

The world and the church need to learn from each other. Passion and purity, sex and chastity, must be brought together.

The church must have the courage to let go of some of its fears and inhibitions here. It must celebrate the goodness of sexuality and challenge people to passion, including sexual passion. As long as the church continues to hesitate it will remain, at one level, the enemy of legitimate delight. Purity makes sense only when linked to passion. Chastity outside the goodness of sexuality is frigidity.

Conversely, the world must relearn purity. It must admit how much of its emotional pain results from trivializing sex, from breaking some of the sacred taboos that surround it, and from denigrating chastity and sexual caution. As long as the world continues to identify purity with naivete, timidity, and Victorian morality, it will remain its own enemy. Passion takes its deeper meaning from purity, sex from chastity.

And this marriage should not be a negotiated fifty-fifty compromise — "passion needs a little purity, sex needs a little chastity." What needs to happen is that each of us, in the world and in the church, must bring together inside us these two deep archetypal pressures (the fire of eros and the desire for innocence).

What will happen then will not resemble the dynamics of a negotiation table but the raging chaos of a storm. A high pressure system will meet a low pressure one and more than a few tornados and thunderstorms will occur. There will be pain and confusion, and settled patterns will be toppled by storm. But through the eye of that storm we will understand life and love as we never have before.

SEX AND SOUL

Recently I was talking with a young woman who was trying to convince me that I, and the church, have a distorted view about sex. "You make it such a big deal and link it so inextricably to love. It can be that, but usually it isn't. I can tell you, most of the time love is not about what happens between the sheets!"

She was talking from considerable experience, and I wasn't about to argue the point. Sex is not always about love, though it should be. It is, however, about soul, and this is the thing that neither my young friend, nor our culture, really understands. Whether it is mindless, abusive, or sacramental, sex always, and deeply, touches soul. Sex and soul are inextricably linked.

Nikos Kazantzakis once wrote:

Three Kinds of Souls, Three Prayers

1. I am a bow in your hands, Lord.
   Draw me, lest I rot.

2. Do not overdraw me, Lord. I shall break.

3. Overdraw me, Lord, and who cares if I break!

Something similar might be said about sex:

Three Kinds of Sex, Three Effects

1. Abusive sex — destroys the soul.

2. Casual sex — trivializes the soul.

3. Sacramental sex — builds up the soul.

In recent years, our culture has come light years forward in its understanding of the first category. We now know how deeply damaging is all sexual abuse. It wounds in a way that perhaps no other thing does. To be violated sexually is not the same as to be violated in other ways. Abusive sex leaves a soul scar that is unique both in its pain and in its power to create chaos and disintegration within the one who has been violated. We now know how deep is the cut that is left by any sexual crime.

Where we have less insight is in our understanding of casual sex. To my mind, there are few areas within human relationships where, as a culture, we are as blind as we are in this one. We live in a culture within which, for the most part, sex has become a normal part of dating and within which we have begun to identify contraceptive responsibility with sexual responsibility. Thus, for the main part, we are beginning to believe that casual sex, "as long as it is consensual, contraceptively responsible, and loving," harms no one and leaves no scars. We rationalize this blindness, as does my young friend, precisely by separating real love from what happens between the sheets.

But while our heads may not be hurt our souls are. They are affected in ways that we no longer have the courage to face squarely. Casual sex, however loving and consensual it pretends to be, trivializes the soul and ultimately cheapens the experience of love. In sex, something very deep is touched, even when it is not intended. It is no accident that past lovers appear in present dreams. Sex and soul are inextricably linked.

The late Allan Bloom, examining this from a purely secular point of view, suggests that casual sex de-eroticizes and demystifies human relationships since sexual passion now no longer includes intimations of eternity. Sex, for all its power and potential, is now "no big deal." In Bloom's words, it, like almost everything else, becomes "narrower and flatter." There can be no illusion of eternity in casual sex. The soul has to make it flat and narrow so as to protect itself against lying. This is a fault in the soul, and the soul that acts in this way is being trivialized and in some way distorted.

Bloom elaborates with a rather graphic example. Lamenting precisely the rather flat and narrow experience of a soul that has been trivialized through its erotic experience, he says: "Plato, in his Symposium, comments on how his students sit around and tell wonderful stories about the meaning of their immortal longings. My own students," says Bloom, "sit around and tell stories of being horny. Such is the difference in soul."

Finally there is sacramental sex. It has power to build up the soul in ways that, this side of eternity, few other experiences can. It is eucharist, incarnation, love-made-flesh, truly. In sacramental sex, a soul is joined to another and in that moment experiences the central purpose of God's design for it. When that happens the soul strengthens and swells, in gratitude, stability, and peace. And that kind of experience of soul is, our culture notwithstanding, truly a big deal.

SEX AND THE SUBLIME

Morris West's novel *The Clowns of God* discusses different views on sexuality. At one point, an older person, with an older view on sex, tells some younger people, with a more contemporary view on sex:

> Nobody can tell you how to arrange your emotional lives, or even your sexual lives. All one can say is that if you waste your hearts and waste that special joy that makes sex so wonderful, it's something you can't renew. . . . You can find other experiences, other joys, too, but never again that first, special very exclusive ecstasy that makes this whole confusion of living and dying worthwhile. (43)

That is fair advice for a generation, ours, which, at least with regard to sex, tends to fight high symbols and high meanings. It is not that we are insincere or have worse morals than past generations, or that we theoretically want to play down the meaning of sexuality. It is that for the most part we neglect that inextricable connection between sublimation and the sublime. We have forgotten the importance of waiting, of longing, of living the sublime fire of tension.

The word "sublime" comes from the word "sublimation." That is no mere accident of language. The sublime depends upon sublimation: to have great satisfaction, there must first be a great effort, to achieve a great peace, there must first have been a great struggle, and to have a great love, there must first have been a great chastity. This is true not just for sexuality, but in every area of life. Great art takes time; nobody creates a masterpiece quickly. Great achievement crowns a great effort; nothing that is truly great is achieved easily. Great satisfaction comes only after great tension; that which comes without resistance gives us no great fulfillment. And powerful ecstasy follows upon painful sublimation; the more soul-wrenching the sublimation, the more soul-exploding the ecstasy.

It is no accident that the great novels within every language are great precisely because they build upon great tension. It is not in passing that Scripture tells us: "Those who sow in tears will reap in joy!" It is not for nothing that the great mystics tell us that the joys of heaven come after a certain "dark night of the soul." It is not without great insight that apocalyptic literature tells us that it is only with much groaning of the flesh that the life of the spirit is brought forth. It is not incidental that God can be born into the world only after a long period of longing. Thus it should not be surprising that many are the saints who stress the importance of chastity, waiting, sublimation.

Our age, for all its unique strengths, tends to have this weakness: it does not understand the sublimity of tension. Hence it has little understanding of nor use for chastity, especially sexual chastity.

We still believe that sex should be sublime but we no longer believe in living the tension that can make it that. We want the sublimity of deep sexuality, but we do not want the painful sublimation upon which it depends. More simply put, we want the ecstasy without the agony, the soul-exploding depth of sex without the soul-building power of chastity.

Sex cannot deliver the goods; it alleviates our loneliness too little, especially our moral loneliness. Sex that isn't sublime doesn't bring us a soul mate. What it brings is a fix, a hit, a drug, that helps us through a lonely night or a lonely season, but that, deep down, we know cannot give us what we need, and sex cannot be sublime without first living a real chastity. The person who sleeps with somebody he or she hardly knows, has no real commitment to, and has never lived a chaste tension with, will not have a sublime or profound experience. Short-circuiting chastity is like trying to write a masterpiece overnight. Good luck, but it isn't going to happen! Great love, like great art, takes great effort, sustained commitment, and lots of time.

Carlo Carretto, one of the great spiritual writers of our time, once spent a number of years living by himself as a hermit, praying in the Sahara desert. When someone asked him what he thought he heard God saying to him in all that silence and after all that prayer, Carretto replied: "God is telling us: learn to wait — wait — wait for your God, wait for love, be patient with everything. Everything that is worthwhile must be waited for!"

Chapter 4

Receive, Give Thanks,
Break, Share

The Eucharist as the Sustenance
of Daily Life

There is an entire spirituality, and Christology, in the four eucharistic words: Receive, Give Thanks, Break, Share.

My belief in the eucharist is simple: without touch, God is a monologue, an idea, a philosophy; he must touch and be touched, the tongue on the flesh, and that touch is the result of monologues, the idea, the philosophies which led to faith, but in the instant of touch there is no place for thinking, for talking, the silent touch affirms all that, and goes deeper. — ANDRE DUBUS, *Broken Vessels*

HOW NOT TO COMMIT
THE ORIGINAL SIN

Some years ago I sat in on a series of lectures on the theology of the Trinity given by James Mackey. At one point in these lectures, Mackey suggested that perhaps the best words available to help us understand somewhat the flow of life within God are the four eucharistic words of Jesus: *receive, give thanks, break,* and *share.*

In explaining the first of these words, "receive," he shared with us a story. A man he knew was once part of a hunting expedition in Africa. One morning this man left the camp early, by himself, and hiked several miles into the jungle, where he surprised and eventually bagged two wild turkeys. Buckling his catch to his belt, he headed back for camp. At a point, however, he sensed he was being followed. With his senses sharpened by fright, he stopped, hands on his rifle, and looked around him. His fears were dispelled when he saw who it was. Following him at a distance was a naked and obviously starved adolescent boy. The boy's objective was food, not threat. Seeing this, the man stopped, unbuckled his belt, and, letting the turkeys fall to the ground, backed off and gestured to the boy that he could come and take the birds. The boy ran up to the two birds but, inexplicably, refused to pick them up. He was, seemingly, still asking for something else. Perplexed, the man tried both by words and by gestures to indicate to the boy that he could have the birds. Still the boy refused to pick them up. Finally, in desperation, unable to explain what he still wanted, the boy backed off several meters from the dead birds and stood with outstretched and open hands ... waiting, *waiting until the man came and placed the birds in his hands*. He had, despite hunger, fear, and intense need, refused to *take* the birds. He waited until they were *given* to him; he received them.

That simple story is a mini-course in fundamental moral theology. It summarizes all of Christ's moral teachings and the entire Ten Commandments. If we, like this boy, would always wait until life was given to us as gift, as opposed to taking it as by right, seizing it, or raping it, we would never break a single commandment. Moreover we would have in our lives the first and most important religious virtue of all, the sense that all is gift, that nothing is owed us by right.

In a way, this story is the opposite of the original sin story. In the Adam and Eve story, God *gives* them life and then adds a commandment which, on the surface, appears rather strange and arbitrary, "Do not eat of the fruit of the tree of knowledge of good and evil." What is this commandment?

In essence, what God is telling Adam and Eve is this: "I am going to *give* you life. You may only *receive* that life. You may *never take* it. To take it is to ruin and destroy the gift that it is." Adam and Eve's sin was, ultimately, one of rape, the act of robbing, despoiling, and taking by force something which can only be had when it is received gratefully and respectfully as gift. Their sin, as is all sin, was an irreverence, the failure to respect the deepest foundations of a reality that is love-contoured. Simply put, the original sin was a failure in gratitude and receptivity, the failure to respect a gift. It is no accident that the author of the story employs images (nakedness, shame) that are suggestive of sexual violation. That is the very point of the story, except that the rape that is being talked about here is wider than sex. In turning away from the posture of receptivity to the posture of seizing, Adam and Eve began to take by force, as by right, what was theirs only as gift. The result of that is always shame, a darkened mind, rationalization, and the beginnings of a dysfunctional world.

In the story of the boy who refused to take the very food he needed to live on, we see what the opposite of original sin looks like. That kind of patient, receptive waiting and respect might aptly be termed "original virtue" — and it is so needed today! In a world whose spirit defines morality by achievement and the accumulation of things, and that invites us to demand our rights and suggests that "God helps those who help themselves," it is radically countercultural to suggest that a patient waiting to be given life (even when we are hungry) is better than the active seizing of it. To Adam and Eve, God said: "It is good, but it is gift, respect it as such. Don't ever *take* the apple!" All of morality is still summarized in that line.

GRATITUDE — THE ULTIMATE VIRTUE

There is a Jewish folk tale which runs something like this:

> There once was a young man who aspired to great holiness. After some time at working to achieve it, he went to see his rabbi.
>
> "Rabbi," he announced, "I think I have achieved sanctity."
>
> "Why do you think that?" asked the rabbi.
>
> "Well," responded the young man, "I've been practicing virtue and discipline for some time now and I have grown quite proficient at them. From the time the sun rises until it sets, I take no food or water. All day long, I do all kinds of hard work for others and I never expect to be thanked. If I have temptations of the flesh, I roll in the snow or in thorn bushes until they go away, and then at night, before bed, I practice the ancient monastic discipline and administer lashes to my bare back. I have disciplined myself so as to become holy."
>
> The rabbi was silent for a time. Then he took the young man by the arm and led him to a window and pointed to an old horse which was just being led away by its master.
>
> "I have been observing that horse for some time," the rabbi said, "and I've noticed that it doesn't get fed or watered from morning to night. All day long it has to do work for people and it never gets thanked. I often see it rolling around in snow or in bushes, as horses are prone to do, and frequently I see it get whipped. But, I ask you: Is that a saint or a horse?"

This is a good parable because it shows how simplistic it is to simply identify sanctity and virtue with self-renunciation and the capacity to do what is difficult. In popular thought there is a common spiritual equation: saint = horse; what is more difficult is always better. But that can be wrong.

To be a saint is to be motivated by gratitude, nothing more and nothing less. Scripture, everywhere and always, makes this point. For example, the sin of Adam and Eve was first and foremost a failure in receptivity and gratitude. God gives them life, each other, and the garden and asks them only to receive it properly, in gratitude — receive and give thanks. The original sin was precisely Adam and Eve's refusal to do this. Instead they took the apple, taking as by right what could only be received gratefully as gift. It is no coincidence that when giving us the eucharist Christ said: "Receive and give thanks." Only after doing this do we go on to "break and share." Before all else, we first give thanks.

To receive in gratitude, to be properly grateful, is the most primary of all religious attitudes. Proper gratitude is ultimate virtue. It defines sanctity. Saints, holy persons, are people who are grateful, people who see and receive everything as gift. The converse is also true. Anyone who takes life and love for granted should not ever be confused with a saint.

Let me try to illustrate this. As a young seminarian, I once spent a week in a hospital, on a public ward, with a knee injury. One night a patient was brought on to our ward from the emergency room. His pain was so severe that his groans kept us awake. The doctors had just worked on him, and it was then left to a single nurse to attend to him. Several times that night, she entered the room to minister to him — changing bandages, giving medication, and so on. Each time, as she walked away from his bed he would, despite his extreme pain, thank her. Finally, after this had happened a number of times, she said to him: "Sir, you don't need to thank me. This is my job!" "Ma'am!" he replied, "it's nobody's job to take care of me! Nobody owes me that. I want to thank you!"

I was struck by that, how, even in his great pain, this man remained conscious of the fact that life, love, care, and everything else come to us as gift, not as owed. He genuinely appreciated what this nurse was doing for him, and he was right — it isn't anybody's job to take care of us!

It is our propensity to forget this that gets us into trouble. The failure to be properly grateful, to take as owed what is offered as a gift, lies at the root of many of our deepest resentments toward others — and their resentments toward us. Invariably when we are angry at someone, especially at those closest to us, it is precisely because we are not being appreciated (that is, thanked) properly. Conversely, I suspect, more than a few people harbor resentments toward us because we, consciously or unconsciously, think that it is their job to take care of us. Like Adam and Eve we take, as if it is ours by right, what can only be received gratefully as gift. This goes against the very contours of love. It is the original sin.

BREAKING THE EUCHARISTIC BREAD

There is a parable about a Cretan peasant that I heard some years ago from John Shea. It runs this way:

> There once lived a peasant in Crete who deeply loved his life. He enjoyed tilling the soil, feeling the warm sun on his naked back as he worked the fields, and feeling the soil under his feet. He loved the planting, the harvesting, and the very smell of nature. He loved his wife and his family and his friends, and he enjoyed being with them, eating together, drinking wine, talking, and making love. And he loved especially Crete, his

beautiful island! The earth, the sky, the sea, it was his!
This was his home.

One day he sensed that death was near. What he
feared was not what lay beyond, for he knew God's
goodness and had lived a good life. No, he feared leaving Crete, his wife, his children, his friends, his home,
and his land. Thus, as he prepared to die, he grasped
in his right hand a few grains of soil from his beloved
Crete and he told his loved ones to bury him with it.

He died, awoke, and found himself at heaven's gates,
the soil still in his hand and heaven's gate firmly barred
against him. Eventually St. Peter emerged through the
gates and spoke to him: "You've lived a good life, and
we've a place for you inside, but you cannot enter unless
you drop that handful of soil. You cannot enter as you
are now!"

The man was reluctant to drop the soil and protested:
"Why? Why must I let go of this soil? Indeed, I cannot!
Whatever is inside those gates, I have no knowledge
of. But this soil, I know...it's my life, my work, my
wife and kids, it's what I know and love, it's Crete!
Why should I let it go for something I know nothing
about?"

Peter answered: "When you get to heaven you will
know why. It's too difficult to explain. I am asking you
to trust, trust that God can give you something better
than a few grains of soil."

But the man refused. In the end, silent and seemingly
defeated, Peter left him, closing the large gates behind.
Several minutes later, the gates opened a second time
and this time, from them, emerged a young child. She
did not try to coax the man into letting go of the soil in
his hand. She simply took his hand and, as she did, it

opened and the soil of Crete spilled to the ground. She then led him through the gates.

A shock awaited him as he entered heaven. There, before him, lay all of Crete!

When Jesus gave us the eucharist, he left it to us with the words: receive, give thanks, break, and share. With these words, he was referring to a lot more than ritual and rubrics for the reception of the eucharist at a liturgy. These words contain an entire spirituality in that they lay out the way that we must live all of life. The story just told helps us to understand what is meant by one of those words, "break."

How do we break so as to become a eucharistic person? Parable and story can touch deep affective levels in us and move us in rationally inexplicable ways, and so a story of this kind should not be given too much explanation. It should be more an object for meditation than explanation. Nonetheless, a tiny application might be helpful.

When Jesus links the idea of breaking to the eucharist, the rending and breaking down that he is talking about have to do with narcissism, individualism, pride, self-serving ambition, and all the other things that prevent us from letting go of ourselves so as to truly be with others. Buddhism suggests that everything that is wrong in the world can be explained in one image, that of the group photo. Whenever anyone looks at a group photo, that person always first looks at how he or she turned out and only afterward considers whether or not it is a good picture of the group. Breaking the eucharistic bread has a whole lot to do with looking first at how the group turned out.

St. Augustine, in his eucharistic sermons, was fond of telling people: "If you receive this well, you are what you receive ... for the loaf that contains Christ is made up of many individual kernels of grain, but these kernels must, to become the loaf containing Christ, first be ground up and then baked together by fire" (*Sermo 227, In Die Paschae IV*).

THE POLISHED STONE

As a young seminarian I spent a summer working in a retreat house. The priest directing the house had a curious hobby: he polished stones. During long, solitary walks he would watch for small stones that looked interesting, and when he found one that looked like it might have value, he would bring it back to his workshop. There he had a small barrel-drum which was itself filled with small, very hard stones. He would take the stone he had found, his potential gem, and place it inside the barrel-drum, add some water, seal the drum tightly, and turn on an electric motor which would slowly rotate the drum. After several weeks of this, he would open the drum and search for his little stone. Many times, he would find that it had disappeared, the weeks of grinding had reduced it to gravel and sand. If the stone, however, had value, he would find it now, polished, gleaming, a gem with all its rough edges rubbed off and all useless gravel and sand knocked out of it.

There is something in that image about family life. There used to be an expression, popular in spiritual literature, that said: families and communities are schools of charity. I remember reading it as a novice many years ago and very naively and very badly misunderstanding it. My simple thought then was: "Yes that makes sense! When you live within a family or some other community, it gives you a lot of chances to practice patience, forgiveness, and understanding — as you deal with other people's faults!" How wrong I was! What that expression suggests is not, first of all, that we grow in charity and maturity by putting up patiently with other people's faults, but that real relationship, actual inter-action within family and community, deflates our fantasies, makes us see reality, punctures our narcissism, and against every protest, denial, and rationalization we can muster, shows us how selfish and immature we often are.

We cannot live very long within any community — mar-riage, family, religious community, or genuine friendship — without becoming aware of our faults and narrowness. We either begin to grow up, or we leave. Sadly, today the temp-tation is most often to leave. The prevalent theory is that we grow mature by growing away, especially away from the fam-ily and community that, by circumstance, we find ourselves within. The idea is that we will be happy — and available for real family and friendship — if we are free spirits, soaring, unattached, unencumbered.

I remember a young nun to whom I once served as spiri-tual director. Before entering the convent, she had lived alone in her own apartment and was quite popular. She had many friends and was, to her own mind, quite a mature, giving, and unselfish person. Not long after joining a religious commu-nity, where she lived in close quarters with other novices and those directing the novitiate, she began to experience major problems with her relationships. She was often at odds with her peers and her directors, who, tactfully and otherwise, told her that she was somewhat self-centered and immature. She was particularly frustrated because often the tensions arose over very petty things.

"It must be the community that's causing this," she told me during one of our sessions. "I was never a petty, selfish person when I lived alone!" Then, when I asked why she continued to stay in the convent if this was the case, she replied: "Because, in my better moments, I know that if I ran off now and got married probably most of the things that are happening here would begin to happen again! Some of this stuff would catch up with me again. When I lived alone it was lonely, but it was easier. You didn't have to live your life under a microscope. But you could easily fool yourself too!"

What was happening to her in that community? The stone was being polished! She was being churned in the barrel-drum that is called family, community. The other stones were knocking some rough edges off of her and rubbing her free of considerable useless gravel and sand. It was painful and humiliating for her, but she was learning the most valuable lesson of all, how to share your life in reality as opposed to fantasy. She was in a school of charity. She was being purified.

Family and community aren't boring; they are terrifying. They're too full of searing revelations; there we have no place to hide. In family life, our selfishness and immaturities are reflected back to us through eyes that are steady and unblinking. Staying within them is often the hell that is purgatory and so leads to heaven.

THANKING THE CREATOR
BY ENJOYING THE GIFT

Several years ago, one of my sisters died of cancer. She was an Ursuline nun, possessed a deep faith, and had for many years given herself over to the service of others with an unselfishness that was exceptional. Yet, despite all this, she found it very hard to die, very hard to let go.

Why? I have seen others, with less faith, let go much more easily. In my sister's case, this was the difficulty: she was not afraid of God, of the afterlife, or of the unknown. This was not the issue. The reason she found it so hard to die was, quite simply, that she loved her life so deeply. She thoroughly loved and enjoyed her life. Friends, work, family, good food, good weather, good chocolate (her weakness), these she basked in. She was not a particularly reflective person, but she was not a moody one either. Her impatience was with those who gave life too much of a tragic or stoic twist. This she considered pompous, false, a waste. Life, for her, was good, something to be drunk in with delight. Her view: to enjoy life is to end up with a double chin. This is what separates the true Christian from the stoic. The formula worked for her. She had a happy life, did eventually develop a double chin, and died a deeply loved woman.

What this story highlights is something that is too often lost within spirituality, namely, that the highest compliment someone can give to a gift giver is to thoroughly enjoy the gift. The highest compliment we can give to God, our Creator, is to thoroughly enjoy the gift of life. One should never look a gift universe in the mouth! The best way to pay for a beautiful moment is to enjoy it.

More often than not, this is not the message that has come through in Christian spirituality, or in virtually every other spirituality and secular philosophy for that matter. Mostly what has been presented as mature, as the ideal to be imitated, is stoicism, the Hamlet-figure, the Socrates-figure, the person who is somehow above and detached from the enjoyments, pleasure, and delights of the ordinary person. A saint who craves chocolate! There aren't many icons, outside Buddhism, that show someone with a double chin. We are the poorer for that. What is not mature is our spiritual understanding. We have mistaken Hamlet for Jesus, stoicism for Christianity, despair for healthy detachment.

This needs correction. The Christian, as John Shea is so fond of pointing out, is not the noble anti-hero, luxuriating in despair, but the child of the kingdom, the grace-merry person who, while sharing fully in the tears of this world, is ultimately distinguished through his or her laughter. To consider life as tragic is to not believe in the resurrection. It is also to not imitate Christ, who shocked as many people with his capacity to enjoy the earth as he did with his challenge to live in the face of the fact that this world is not our true home.

I was taught this lesson by Gustavo Gutiérrez, the father of liberation theology. I was once fortunate enough to meet him. He is a man with a passion for justice, but he is also a man with passion for life. I remember an incident some years back when he came to deliver some lectures at the college where I was teaching. My job was to pick him up from the airport, take him to breakfast, and get him settled in. I guided him into my car with considerable trepidation for, in my mind, I was transporting an icon. That feeling, unfair as it was, disappeared when I took him to breakfast in our college cafeteria. He wasn't a pious icon, he was man, and he was a man who thoroughly enjoyed his breakfast! After loading his plate with a generous sample of everything that our cooks had laid out, he sat down to table, said a grace, and then made the pronouncement: "I like eating! When I was a child there often wasn't enough food. Now, when there is, I thoroughly enjoy it!" He enjoyed good food without apology. He also had the beginnings of a double chin. Hardly what you expect from the father of liberation theology! But, then, people didn't expect that of Jesus either!

Passing strange, yet strangely true, it is invariably those who see and live out most clearly the fact that this world is not our true home who also have the ability to enjoy life most fully. Occasionally too they have double chins. My sister would have liked Gutiérrez. They would have enjoyed chocolate together.

The best way to thank a gift giver is to thoroughly enjoy the gift.

EUCHARIST
AS GOD'S TOUCH

Andre Dubus, in a beautiful essay on the eucharist, includes the comment quoted at the head of this chapter. Like that of Dubus, my belief in the eucharist is also simple: the eucharist is God's physical embrace of us, God's touch. Nowhere is the body of Christ so physical, sensual, carnal, and available for deep intimacy as in the eucharist. Lest this type of talk scandalize, it might be well to read St. Paul's thought on the matter. Speaking of our union with Christ and with each other within Christ's body, Paul points out that it is as real, as physical, and as sensual as is the union of sexual intercourse. Today we do not take seriously enough this radical physical and sensual character of the eucharist. Rarely do we risk understanding the eucharist in the earthy terms which I will propose here. We are the poorer for it.

The early church was less reticent than we are. For it, the eucharist was a communion of such deep physical intimacy that they surrounded it with a certain secrecy and barred all except the fully initiated from being there. They practiced something they called the *disciplina arcani.* Part of this discipline was the practice of never speaking about the eucharist to anyone except to fully initiated Christians and to not allow anyone who was not fully initiated to attend the eucharistic celebration. Our present practice within the RCIA of asking catechumens to leave after the homily is based upon this ancient discipline.

This secrecy, however, was not an attempt to surround the eucharist with a certain mystique so as to intrigue others to be curious about it, as is usually the case with secrecy of this kind. It was not an attempt to create some secret cult. The secrecy was a reverence. For them the eucharist was such an intimate thing that one did not do it with just anyone, nor did one talk about it publicly — akin to not making love in public and being too exhibitionist about your intimacies. In their view, in the eucharist you made love — and that is done with the bedroom door closed.

The shrouding of the eucharist with this kind of quasi-sexual reverence is in fact most proper. In the eucharist, Christ touches us, intimately, physically, sensually, carnally. Eucharist is physical, not spiritual; its embrace is real, as physical as the incarnation itself.

In this way, eucharist is more radical than is the Word. Indeed the relationship of the Word to the eucharist is most accurately, and profitably, understood within the metaphor of physical embrace and sexual intercourse (and this may be more than metaphor). The Word is sacramental, but it is less physical than the eucharist. The communion it creates is less physical than eucharistic union. In a manner of speaking, the Word is a preparation for, a readying for, making love. Its role is to prepare us for eucharistic communion. The eucharist is the touch, the physical coming together, the embrace, the consummation, the intercourse.

I suspect that this kind of comparison might scandalize and upset some people. Comparing the intimacy of eucharistic communion to sexual intercourse, isn't this going a bit far? It is going far, admittedly; but it errs primarily in the fact that it does not go far enough. The mystery of the Body of Christ — God becoming incarnate, Christ leaving us the Word and the eucharist, and the intimacy and communion that we experience with Christ and each other in the eucharist — can, in the end, not be exaggerated. Its reality, including its physical character, goes further than we imagine. This is not wild new theory; it is wild old doctrine. Pius XII said as much in *Mystici Corporis*.

A friend of mine, a recent convert, is fond of saying: "I became a Catholic because of the eucharist. I don't really understand it, but I feel, always, its reality and power. Nothing is more precious to me." The eucharist is more than sufficient reason to become a Catholic, or indeed a Christian of any denomination. To be embraced physically by God is, on either side of eternity, all that one can hope for. Like Andre Dubus, I long, daily, for that kind of touch.

GOD, FORGIVENESS, AND THE EUCHARIST

Recently a man came to me with a confession. With his permission, I share it with you.

Father, I come not so much to ask for forgiveness as to celebrate the forgiveness that God has already given to me. Until this past Sunday, I had been away from the church for nineteen years. I grew up in a very strict Catholic family in a rural area. My mother was very religious and my father was very rigid and strict. I hated him and all he stood for and left home at seventeen. I enjoyed the freedom of living in a big city and soon let myself go sexually. Within a year, I was no longer going to church or praying. I also began to resent more and more both my father and the Catholic Church. In my mind, they both stood for the same thing — repression and control of others' lives.

For nearly nineteen years this resentment deepened and I never went to church, nor did I go home, except for family weddings, and then I made sure that I was never alone with my dad. During these nineteen years, I never married, remained sexually active, and had oc-

casional bursts of religious fervor when I would attend
some Protestant churches. Each time I went back to
church, I felt that I had finally found my religious place.
But each time I eventually drifted off again, back to my
old sexual habits and my resentments of the Catholic
Church and my dad.

A little more than a year ago, I had a conversion.
Initially, it had nothing to do with religion. My lover
left me and I was devastated, almost suicidal. I couldn't
break the obsession and, at the edges of a breakdown, I
decided to change my lifestyle. At first this change had
only to do with a change in my relational and sexual
life. I began to build my life in such a way that I might
someday have a relationship that would be based upon
permanent commitment and fidelity. After about six
months, just as I was starting to find my strength again,
I realized, at some dark place in me, that my struggle
to find that new lifestyle involved my being reconciled
with my dad and with the church of my youth.

With a lot of fear, I went home to visit my father. It
was a bitter, tearful, and, eventually, reconciling visit. I
spent a whole summer at home (giving up my job here
in the process), but it was worth it. My dad died a month
after I left to come back here and I will, for as long as I
live, be grateful we had those three months together.

When I got back here, I decided to go back to church.
Initially, I went to see a priest and asked him whether,
having been away from the church for so long and having been at odds with its teachings concerning marriage
and sexuality, it would be okay if I just went back to
church and to communion? He said no and told me I
must first go to confession. Angered, I left and began
again to attend a non-Catholic church. But, at a point,

I realized that what I really *wanted and needed* was the eucharist, communion.

The next Sunday, I just did it! I simply went to a Catholic church, attended mass, and went to communion. I don't care what the rules are, but I know I did right. I can only describe what happened in that communion as feeling "washed in the blood of Christ," forgiven of everything, stripped of bitterness and anger, and set free in a way that, I know, no private prayer, prayer group, service of the word, or psychological counseling could ever approximate. I was forgiven. There was a tremendous psychological rush, but that, I know, can be superficial. At a deeper level, at that level where you *just know* things, I knew that I was forgiven and that I had done the right thing. Funny thing, the priest I had talked to said I couldn't go to communion until I'd first gone to confession. Then everything inside of me resisted confession. Now, when I know I've been forgiven, I *want* and I *need* to go to confession. That's why I am here.

What this story highlights is something the church has always taught, even in its official teachings, and which (because we are so bound up with Jansenism and Pelagianism) we invariably lose, namely, that *the eucharist is the primary sacrament of reconciliation* and that *going to eucharist is not a moral statement:* We go to eucharist because we *need* health, not because we *are* healthy. One of the great tragedies is that, inevitably, when we need eucharist the most, when we most need to touch the body of Christ because of the moral and psychological mess we find ourselves in, we stay away because we think (or have been told) that to go to communion we must *first* put our lives in order.

It highlights too even a more significant point: God's *forgiveness, unlike our own, is lavish, scandalous, unmeasured, unmemoried, and beyond all exacting and recriminations.* And we are self-righteous and not living in God's righteousness when we squirm at this and consider it "cheap grace." God's ways truly are not our ways! Nowhere is this more true than in the lavishness and unconditionality of God's forgiveness. The God who is the transcendent Creator of all the universes — accessible as the nearest water tap!

Chapter 5

A Good Fireplace, a Warm House, Moral Companionship, and Sacramental Sex

The Sacrament of Marriage

Thomas came to this conclusion: making love with a woman and sleeping with a woman are two separate passions, not merely different but opposite. Love does not make itself felt in the desire for copulation (a desire that extends to an infinite number of women) but in the desire for shared sleep (a desire limited to one woman).
— MILAN KUNDERA, *The Unbearable Lightness of Being*

Yet something remains
the dream of fewness
one woman, one man.
— J. S. PORTER,
The Thomas Merton Poems

IMAGES OF A MARRIAGE

No amount of preaching shapes a soul as much as does the influence of a good Christian life. If that is true, and it is, then no marriage course is ever as powerful to teach about marriage as is the witness of a good marriage.

I understood this, firsthand, a few weeks ago when I attended the fiftieth wedding anniversary of an uncle and an aunt. Theirs has been a good marriage — good harmony, good hospitality, good family, sustained faith. However, and only they know the full price tag, this did not always come easily. They spent enough years without money and without extras, raising a large family. His first job, clerking in a store, paid him fifty cents a day. She couldn't find any work at all — "women weren't needed in the job market in those days!" There were as well, as in all families, countless other struggles and, in their case, countless more hours spent, by both, beyond their own family concerns, working in church and community circles.

Nearly three hundred of us, family and friends, gathered to toast and roast them. At the end of the banquet my uncle stood up to thank everyone. He ended his comments with the words: "When we got married fifty years ago, we didn't have much, but we had an unconscious trust that if we lived by the Ten Commandments and the laws of the church then things would turn out all right...and I think they did."

What an understatement! They turned out more than all right. A good marriage can best be described, I believe, by four images and theirs is the prime analogue of each of these:

- A good marriage is a warm *fireplace*. The love that two people have for each other generates a warm place. But the warmth it creates does not warm just the two people in love; it warms everyone else who comes near them — their children, their neighbors, their community, and everyone who meets them.

- A good marriage is a big *table, loaded with lots of food and drink*. When two people love each other sacramentally that love becomes a place of hospitality, a table where people come to be fed — figuratively and really. Again, love, in a true marriage, feeds not just the two people who are generating it, but, because it is sacramental, it always contains more than enough surplus to feed everyone who is fortunate enough to meet it.

- A good marriage is a *container that holds suffering*. An old axiom says: "Everything can be borne if it can be shared!" That's true. Anyone fortunate enough to have a true moral partner in this life can bear a lot of suffering. That is even more true in a good marriage where the wife and husband, because of their deep moral and emotional affinity, can carry not just their own sufferings but also can help carry the sufferings of many others.

- Finally, to draw upon a deep Christian image, a good marriage *is Christ's body*, flesh that is "food for the life of the world." Christ left his body to feed the world. A good marriage does precisely that, it feeds everything and everybody around it. Many of us have experienced this in some of the married people we have met. Having them in our lives is a constant source of moral, psychological, religious, and humorous nourishment.

The marriage of my aunt and uncle is, exactly, described by these images. Their relationship to each other is a *fireplace* where many people, including myself, have found warmth. It is a *table* — all their houses have always had big tables, big loaded refrigerators, and big doors that have welcomed and given hospitality and food and drink to everyone who crossed their threshold. And their relationship has been a *container for suffering*. Through the years, thanks to their love for each other, they were able to bear with faith, dignity, soft hearts, and ever-deepening charity all the pain, tragedy, and suffering that came their way. But they were also able to help many other people, including my own family when we lost our parents, to carry their sufferings. Finally, their relationship has been, and remains, *Christ's body, food for the life of the world.* Virtually everyone whose path ever crossed theirs has been fed, nourished, given vitamins in their soul by this marriage.

An age that no longer understands sacrament, might, I submit, look at a marriage like this one to better see what shapes a soul and what constitutes a sacrament. Sometimes the answers we seek are not found in books but in the house across the street. Sometimes too the sacrament we need to feed our souls is found, not just at the communion rail, but in a warm living room and at a loaded table.

TWO AS ONE FLESH

This summer one of my sisters died. As much as we all miss her, none of us, including her own children, feels her absence as much as her husband. He doesn't just miss her. Half his life is gone. That is where he is different from her kids: they lost their mum, but still have a whole self left. He wakes up mornings, walks through days, and goes about the business of raising family and crops with some of his own body missing. That is no romantic exaggeration, as everyone who knew them knows. They were married, husband and wife for thirty-four years, and everything about them and their relationship suggested that what was between them was rare.

"And the two shall be one flesh!" That they were, just as the second page of the Bible describes it. Both had left their own families, and a lot of other things, to cling to each other, to be one flesh. When a man and a woman love each other in that way, truly in that way, each dies and something new, some third thing, is born. In my sister and brother-in-law's relationship, you saw this third thing, human love consummated, grown sacramental. Small wonder that my brother-in-law now feels only half alive. For a while he

had an ally, a co-conspirator, against the most primal of all loneliness, the one that God himself damned at the origins of history: "It is not good for the man to be alone!" For a time, he was not alone. He was married — married in a way that is worth reflecting upon.

What makes a great marriage? What made my sister and her husband "one flesh" in a way that is so often denied the rest of us? What really marries one person to another? There are all kinds of answers to these questions and, given a culture that constellates so many of its feelings about love around sex and romantic obsession, what was true in their case is normally not what comes first to mind. They weren't Romeo and Juliet. Theirs was not the stuff of Hollywood romances and Iris Murdoch novels. What was so special between them could easily be missed. It had such a quietness to it, a gentleness, softness, and chastity, that it contained nothing of those exaggerated forms that make for great art — and often for tumult, heartbreak, and infidelity in real life. Nothing between them garbled life. Their relationship was, for the most part, too ordinary to notice. They didn't often get the chance to look at each other over crystal wine glasses under romantic lighting, though they yearned for that. They had to catch each other's eye more domestically. For whole years at a stretch, over dirty diapers and dirty dishes, in a house packed with kids, they would meet each other's eyes and both would know that they were home: "At last, bone from my bone, flesh from flesh." They knew what consummation meant. For thirty-four years they had only to look at each other to not be alone.

But what makes this? What needs to be there for someone to look at another and feel that other as bone from my bone, flesh from my flesh, kindred spirit? In today's terminology, what makes someone a soul mate? What do you need to experience with another person to overcome that exile of heart?

Someone looking at my sister and brother-in-law might, more superficially, have seen some obvious things: deep mutual respect, a gentleness between them, uncompromising fidelity to each other, harmony of thought and feelings on most things important, regular prayer together, and a complete trust of each other. Those things are the heart of a marriage. But, in the end, these were, in their case, symptoms really. What connected them, made for bone of my bone, for the harmony, respect, fidelity, and gentleness was something deeper. They had moral affinity. Long before, and concomitant with, sleeping with each other physically, they slept with each other morally.

What's meant by this curious phrase? Each of us has a place inside where we feel most deeply about the right and wrong of things and where what is most precious to us is cherished and guarded. It is when this place is attacked that we feel most violated. It is also the place where, in the end, we feel most alone. More deeply than we long for a sexual partner, we long for someone to sleep with us here.

My sister and brother-in-law found this in each other. They were moral lovers. They found, touched, and protected each other's souls. Everything that was deepest and most precious in each of them was understood, cherished, and safe when the other was around. It made for a great marriage — one flesh, true consummation, all predicated on a great trust and a great chastity. This is a secret worth knowing.

SEX AS SACRAMENT

A Catholic journalist recently commented that the world will begin to take the church seriously when it talks about sex if the church, first of all, affirms what it should always be affirming, namely, that for married persons the marriage bed is their daily eucharist.

Sex as a sacrament. Sex as eucharist. Is this high spiritual truth or is it blasphemy? It can be either since, within a Christian understanding, sex is precisely either sacrament or perversity. In a recent article in *Grail* British psychiatrist Jack Dominion discusses the sacramental role of sex within a marriage. Without denying what traditional Christian thought has always affirmed, that is, that procreation is a function of married sexuality, he goes on to suggest five possibilities (ultimately, sacramental possibilities) which can be realized each time a married couple make love.

First, each time they do make love they, potentially, verify their personal significance to each other. More simply put, each act of sexual intercourse is a reminder (and a celebration) of the fact that they are the most important person in each other's lives. Sexual intercourse, within its proper context, love consecrated through marriage, verifies and celebrates (physically, emotionally, and spiritually) what was pronounced in their marriage vows, namely, "My love is now consecrated, displaced, for you!"

Dietrich Bonhoeffer once told a couple he was marrying: "Today you are young and very much in love. You think that your love will sustain your marriage. Well, I give you the opposite advice — let your marriage sustain your love." Sexual orgasm facilitates a personal encounter that speaks of and demands precisely the type of exclusiveness and fidelity that the marriage vows promise.

Second, sexual intercourse is one of the most powerful acts through which a couple reinforce each other's sexual identity, making, as Dominion puts it, the woman feel fully feminine and the man fully masculine.

Third, sexual intercourse can be, potentially, a most power-ful act of reconciliation, healing, and forgiveness. In all relationships, perhaps especially in married ones, wounds will appear (arising from, among other things, different tem-peraments, disappointment with each other, past histories, weaknesses, and inadequacies) which will, at one level, ap-pear to create an unbridgeable chasm. Sexual orgasm can facilitate a peak experience within which harmony is restored beyond the hurt, not because the hurt is taken away, but be-cause in that peak experience something is felt which, for a second at least, lets persons drop the load of hurt, disap-pointment, and bitterness and meet in a super-reconciliation which is a foretaste of the reconciliation of heaven itself.

Fourth, sexual intercourse is perhaps, singularly, the most powerful way a couple has of telling each other that they wish to continue in this consecrated relationship. Freud once said we understand the structure of a thing by looking at it when it is broken. Thus we see that within a marriage when the sexual bond is broken, when there is an unwillingness or a hesitancy to sleep with each other, there is, at some level, also some unwillingness or hesitancy to continue the relationship at a very deep level.

Finally, sexual intercourse is, as Dominion so aptly puts it, a rich vein of thanksgiving. Orgasm, within a proper relationship, spawns gratitude.

Given these possibilities for sex, it does not strain the imagination to see that the marriage bed is, potentially, a sacrament, a daily eucharist. A sacrament is, as theol-ogy has always said in one fashion or another, someone or something that visibly prolongs a saving action of Christ; something visible, fleshy, tangible, incarnate, that somehow makes God present. More specifically still, what takes place in the marriage bed (between a couple who are properly loving each other) parallels what takes place between ourselves and Christ in the eucharist. Each eucharist also has those five possibilities: In that encounter we say to Christ and Christ says to us: "My life is consecrated, displaced, for you." Through that encounter, as well, we reinforce our identity as Christians, are embraced in a super-reconciliation, announce through word and action that we want to continue in a deep relationship with Christ, and are imbued with and express gratitude.

The marriage bed, like the eucharist, is fleshy, tangible, visible, and incarnate. (Not at all a sacrament for angels!) Like the eucharist too it expresses special love, fidelity, reconciliation, and gratitude in an earthy way. That quality, its earthiness, makes it, like the eucharist, a very powerful and privileged sacrament. Through it the word becomes flesh and dwells among us.

BLESSING HOUSES AND HOUSES THAT BLESS

Recently I was invited by a young couple to bless their new home. This custom, blessing houses, is not exactly fashionable today, both because we move so often that we rarely see our houses as something worth blessing and because blessings in general are often considered as something overly pious, a near superstition left over from a former religious time. Former generations used to have their houses blessed as a form of protection. A blessing, it was then believed, helped ward off the devil, lightning storms, prowlers, and every other kind of evil. Today we tend to get other kinds of insurances against these things. So why bless our houses? That question was on my mind as I set out, complete with a ritual book of blessings in hand, to bless my friends' house. But there was something else on my mind too, something that invariably appears in my mind whenever I am asked to bless a house, namely, the house that I grew up in. From the way that house has blessed me through the years, I have some dim sense of what kind of blessing a house can give us, if we, first of all, bless it.

I grew up in an immigrant farming community. We were a large family and lived in a small two-story farmhouse. Soon after marrying and setting out on their own, my parents had bought an old shack-type farmhouse and then, as finances allowed, twice enlarged and remodeled that house until it took the shape that it had when I was a young child. It wasn't a luxurious house by any stretch of the imagination. It had no indoor plumbing, bad central heating, and barely enough space for so large a family. But it was snug, real snug, and as a child, surrounded always by so many family members, I always felt secure in that house. It was indeed a home, our place, my place, a place where I was away from the world. Perhaps that phrase best captures the feelings of that house, of any real home: it's a place where you're away from the world. It's your place to be comfortable in, to be sick in, to fight with your family in, to cry in, to dream both night dreams and daydreams in, to be snug in. That is what it means to be at home, and the house I grew up in gave me that security.

I remember especially the feelings I sometimes had on certain winter days, when it was too cold and stormy for the school bus to operate and we would stay home from school. Few of my memories are as warm and precious as those. The cold wind raging outside, all of the elements so fierce and hostile, and me inside, secure and surrounded by family, warm and snug, smelling the wood stove and my mother's cooking as I lounged on my bed or pushed my face against a frosted window to stare at the blizzard. What was happening outside, the cold, snow, and wind, highlighted the warmth and safety of that house. I was as warm and safe as a baby inside the womb — and, on those stormy days, almost as peaceful and secure.

Our family still owns that house — which has now undergone a third remodeling — and through my adult years there have been many times when I have left my present home and place of work and set out for that house, full of tension, dissipation, insecurity, and every kind of restlessness, and soon after arriving there found myself slowly, imperceptibly, growing steady and calm. It's nearly infallible, when I walk into that house, I grow steadier, gain calm, become more sure of who I am, such is its magic. A good house can do that for you. It is for this reason that we should bless our houses, and it is for this kind of grace we should ask when we do bless them.

When I blessed my friends' house, I didn't ask, first of all, that this blessing ward off the devil, lightning storms, natural catastrophes, and prowlers. It is not that these are not real or important or that I believe our age to be above praying for help of this kind. No, it is just that these things are secondary to what really needs to be asked for when one blesses a house.

What do you ask for when you bless a house? I asked that God make this house for them, precisely, a shelter from storms, a place of calm, of peace, of steadiness, a place within which they and their children can comfortably rest, eat, sleep, fight, get sick, and enjoy themselves when a blizzard keeps them home. I asked too that it be a place where they could smell warmth, like people used to smell the wood burning in their kitchen stoves. I asked that it be, for them, a home, a safe place, warm and snug, safe as a mother's womb.

THE TRADITIONAL IDEA OF
LOVE AND MARRIAGE — UNDER SIEGE

Most of us who are over thirty-five were raised on a certain morality regarding marriage, sex, and family. In brief, we were taught the ideal of one sexual and marriage partner for life. We didn't always live up to this ideal, but, if we didn't, we saw that failure as a certain falling away, a fracturing of the norm. Moreover, this was not just something that we felt was morally nonnegotiable; it was our romantic ethos and part of the very infrastructure of Western imagination. Not only did our churches teach this; our romantic novels glorified it.

Today that concept, that the ideal way to express sexual love is within a lifelong married commitment, is under siege. The challenge comes first of all from practical life, where more and more the norm is not sex inside of marriage and lifelong commitments, but sex outside of marriage, infidelity within marriage, divorce as normal, and various forms of temporarily living together in noninstitutionalized and non-sacramentalized ways. More significantly perhaps, this ideal is being challenged theoretically, both as a moral model and as a romantic ethos. An example of this is *Revolution Within*, by Gloria Steinem, in which she suggests that the old moral and romantic idea of marriage and the place of sex within it is both flawed and harmful. Among other things she argues that its basis is not morality or true romanticism, but an unfortunate historical accident which (she more than hints) religion helped bring about for its own fearful and patriarchal purposes.

> We still think of love as "happily ever after." That was a myth even in the nineteenth century, when, as Margaret Mead pointed out, marriage worked better because people only lived to be fifty. (Charlotte Bronte [who

idealized romantic love] herself died at thirty-nine of toxemia during her first pregnancy.) Though an average life span is now thirty years longer in many countries of the world, we haven't really accepted the idea of loving different people at different times, in different ways. It's possible to raise children with a loved partner and then move amicably on to a new stage of life, to love someone and yet live apart, to forge new relationships at every phase of life, even at the very end — in short, to enjoy different kinds of love, in a way that doesn't hurt but only enriches. [Love has such resiliency, here she quotes Alice Walker, that] the new face I turn up to you no one else on earth has ever seen. (282–83)

Futurist Alvin Toffler and many other social analysts today suggest roughly the same thing.

What is to be said about this? Is the old moral and romantic idea of marriage, in the end, dysfunctional and repressive? Could Christianity morally sanction a whole different way of living out sexuality and marriage? Should our romantic imagination be radically restructured?

Hegel suggested that thought makes progress through dialectics. We have today, both practically and theoretically, an antithesis to our classical idea of sex and marriage. Steinem's expression simply articulates what millions of people today in fact believe and live. Are they right? My own belief (and I say this categorically) is that they are not, neither morally nor romantically. However, despite this their critique offers things that need to be integrated, as an antithesis, within the classical view of sex and marriage.

Where it is corrective morally is in its insistence that love and sexuality are complex, evolving, and almost infinitely resilient. Sometimes we didn't emphasize that sufficiently in the past, namely, that falling from the ideal of love leaves scars that are permanent, but not fatal, that love gives us more than one chance in this life, and that we are asked to deeply love more than one person, even within the ideal of monogamy, lifelong commitment, and sex only within marriage — and not everyone who doesn't fit the norm or who has fallen from it is tainted, fallen, second best, or (like the rich young man) must go away sad. Romantically it also offers something positive, namely, not to put so much stock in the Romeo and Juliet ideal (one man and one woman, destined from all eternity to be salvation and wholeness to each other) so as to render real marriage an institution which can only chronically disappoint.

God writes straight with crooked lines. In the current antithesis to the traditional idea of sex and marriage there is a positive moral and romantic challenge.

BUT ARE HEARTS INFINITELY STRETCHABLE?

The notion that the only proper way to fully express sexual love is within a lifelong marriage is today under siege, both as a moral and a romantic ideal. Not only is practical life challenging it, but many respected analysts are suggesting that the old ideas of sex only within marriage and marriage for a lifetime are historically and socially conditioned notions that life and evolution have now rendered obsolete.

Alvin Toffler, for example, remarks how some of the young people at Woodstock (over thirty years ago already) told him that they practiced free love there because "we'll never see any of these people again, so it's okay! It's not like our lives are irrevocably tied together. In a situation like this, sex is not something that follows a long process of relationship-building.

It's a shortcut to deeper communication!" Toffler suggests that, given the high degree of mobility and transience within Western society today, perhaps what was true at Woodstock can now be true for the population at large. The former morality and mystique surrounding sex and marriage, he intimates, made more sense in a culture of little change. Gloria Steinem is suggesting roughly the same thing — the old ideas of sex and marriage are, for most people today, obsolete. I have just suggested that this critique is not without its merits. Here, however, I want to examine its more negative underside.

Steinem, in her call for an end to the old absolutes regarding sex and marriage, submits that we can move on to a new paradigm within which sex can be given ideal expression outside marriage and within which people can move on to new partners as they move on to new phases in their lives. This, she suggests, can be done in a way that "doesn't hurt but only enriches." She illustrates this with her own story: Some years ago she met a man; they fell in love, became friends, then lovers, and then, after some years, both moved on to take on other lovers — but, at the same time, were able to retain a deep and life-giving relationship with each other. She holds this up as a possible paradigm for what love, sex, and romance might be within a new order.

I am not one to dispute her experience, but I am one to claim that it is most *atypical.* What she describes rarely happens in such a way that it "doesn't hurt but only enriches." More often it leaves in its wake a broken heart, a broken life, bitterness, jealousy, emptiness, suicidal restlessness, and depression. The human heart and the human psyche are evolving and resilient, but they have limits regarding how much they can stretch and what they can healthily absorb. Feelings of fierce jealousy, bitter anger, and obsessive depression at losing a relationship are not just culturally conditioned responses. If they are then the great novelists and poets (Shakespeare, Tolstoy, Dostoyevsky, Kundera, Lessing, Browning, among others) are both wrong and naive. Hearts don't break through lack of enlightenment. They break when the contours of love are violated, when something unbending within them is bent. Fractured relationships, irrespective of the personal maturity of those who suffer them, often cause precisely this kind of bending. "The heart has its reasons," Pascal suggests. Love and sex have their own inner dictates, many of which are a mystery to the understanding. There are aspects of love and sex that simply do not evolve and move on, save for the tearing out of some deep roots within the heart. To suggest that this is not true is to ignore human experience.

Entirely independent of religious considerations, though these might fruitfully be considered, one must be careful in throwing away the old links between sex and marriage and between marriage and lifelong commitment. The anger, bitterness, jealousy, depression, chaos, and not-so-quiet desperation that almost always surround the "evolution to new relationships" are not so much a sign that we need a new paradigm for understanding sex and love as they are the heart's protest.

The thesis that love and sex are infinitely adaptable, that they have no inherent boundaries that demand a certain exclusivity and fidelity in their most intimate expressions, might be an expression of faith in the evolutionary potential of humanity, but, in the end, it is mistaken, both in terms of morality and romance — and is, I submit, more naive than the naivete of traditional morality and romance that it seeks to enlighten. The heart has its reasons. It also has its limits. The old morality of sex and marriage, I believe, protected that insight.

GOD IS THE REAL PARENT

Toward the end of the movie *Rachel, Rachel,* there is a particularly moving dialogue. Rachel, the story's main character, an aging spinster teacher, is more than a little frustrated with her state in life: teaching other people's children rather than having her own. Lamenting to another woman, who is a mother, she complains how difficult it is for her as a teacher to work intimately with and get to know the young children in her classroom only to have them soon move on to other classrooms and to grow away from her. She expresses an honest envy of women who have their own children. The mother, to whom she is speaking, says in reply: "It's not so different for a parent. You also get to have young children only for a short time. They move on and grow away from you. They have their own lives and don't belong to you. In the end, even for parents, your kids are never really your own!"

There is much to be learned from meditating on that: the children we have are not really ours. They are given to us, in trust, for a time, a short time really, and we are asked to be mothers and fathers, stewards, mentors, guardians, teachers, and friends to them, but they are never really our children. They belong to somebody else — God — and to themselves more than they ever belong to us. There is both a deep challenge and a deep consolation in understanding and accepting that. The challenge is more obvious. If we accept this, we will be less inclined to act as "owners," to manipulate our children for our own needs, to see them as satellites within our own orbits, and more inclined to love, cajole, challenge, and correct, even while giving them their freedom. The consolation is not as obvious: when we realize that our children, in the healthy sense, are not really ours, we also realize that we are not alone in raising and caring for them. We are, in the end, foster parents. God is the real parent, and God's love, care, aid, and presence to our children is always in excess of our own. God's anxiety for our children is also deeper than our own.

Ultimately, you are never a single parent, even when you don't have a human spouse to help you. God, like you, is also worrying, struggling, involved, crying tears of solicitousness, trying to awaken love. What is consoling is that God can touch, challenge, soften, and inspire at levels inside a child that you cannot reach. Moreover, your children cannot, ultimately, turn their backs on God. They can refuse to listen to you, walk away from you, spit on your values, but there is always another parent from whom they can never walk away, whom they carry inside. Nobody, I suspect, could ever have the courage to be a parent without realizing this.

That we are not alone in our task of parenting needs emphasis today for another reason. More and more, very sincere couples are opting not to have children for fear of the world into which they would be bringing those children. They look at the world, at themselves, their inadequacy and are frightened at what they see: "Do we really want to bring children into a world like this? We are powerless to guarantee them health, safety, security, love. It's an unfair risk to the child!" Persons who think like this are right in their feeling of powerlessness and in their sense that they cannot guarantee health, safety, love, and security to a potential child. But they are wrong in their feeling that they alone are responsible for effecting and guaranteeing these. God is also there and, because of that, in the end all will be well and all manner of being will be well. One can risk having children since God risks it.

Finally, and perhaps most consoling of all, realizing this can do more than a little to bring back some peace and joy into the hearts of those who have lost children tragically to accidents, but especially to suicide, drug- and alcohol-related deaths, and other such things that make parents second-guess, worry about their failures and betrayals, and worry about the things they should have done. Again, we are being asked to not forget that we are not the only parents here. When this child died, in whatever circumstances, that child was received by hands far gentler than our own. They left our foster care and our inadequacy to live with a parent who can fully embrace them and bring them to joy and wholeness.

Parents and prospective parents: fear not, you are inadequate! But there is some good news: you are not alone!

Chapter 6

From Womb to Womb, Mother to Mother

Mortality, Death, Resurrection

Stop all the clocks, cut off the telephone,
Prevent the dog from barking with a juicy bone.
Silence the pianos and with muffled drum
Bring out the coffin, let the mourners come.
— W. H. AUDEN, *Twelve Songs*

There is such a thing as a good death. We ourselves are responsible for the way we die. We have to choose between clinging to life in such a way that death becomes nothing but a failure, or letting go of life in freedom so that we can be given to others as a source of hope.... The real question before our death, then, is not, how much can I still accomplish, or how much influence can I still exert? but, how can I live so that I can continue to be fruitful when I am no longer here among my family and friends? That question shifts our attention from doing to being. Our doing brings success, but our being bears fruit.
— HENRI NOUWEN, *Life of the Beloved and Our Greatest Gift*

AN OLD MONK'S QUESTION

Recently, while I was giving a retreat at a Trappist monastery, an old monk came to talk to me. He shared with me at length the ups and downs of more than fifty years of monastic life. At the end of all that he said to me: "Give me some hints on how I should prepare to die! What should I do to make myself more ready for death?"

The bluntness and heaviness of that question is, of itself, enough to intimidate a person with a spirituality deeper than my own, but when it is asked by someone twice your age whose heart and spirit seem already deeply charitable, faith-filled, and well mellowed out through years of quiet prayer, then perhaps one's best response is silence. I was not so naive as to offer him much by way of an answer, his eagerness notwithstanding. But his is a good question. Indeed, how can we prepare to die? How should we live so that death does not catch us unaware, "as a thief in the night"? What should we do so that we do not leave this world with too much unfinished business?

The first thing that needs to be said in response to these questions is that anything we do to prepare for death must, if it is not to be a morbid and sick thing, be something that does not distance us or separate us from life and others here and now. We do not prepare for death through any kind of withdrawal. The very opposite is true. What prepares us for death, anoints us for it, in Christ's phrase, is a deeper, more intimate, and fuller entry into life. We get ready for death by beginning to live life as we should have been living it all along. I would like to flesh this out by quoting two phrases from two of my favorite authors: John Shea and John Powell.

In his poem "The Indiscriminate Host" John Shea writes: *The banquet is open to all who are willing to sit down with all.* There is a whole lot contained in that line. What Shea suggests here is that the single condition for going to heaven is to have the kind of heart and the kind of openness that make it possible for us to sit down with absolutely anyone — and to share life and a table with anyone. For Shea, then, the best way we can prepare to die is to begin to stretch our hearts to love ever wider and wider, to begin to love in a way that takes us beyond the natural narrowness and discrimination that exists within our hearts because of temperament, wound, timidity, ignorance, selfishness, race, religion, circumstance, and our place in history. We prepare to die by pushing ourselves to love less narrowly. In that sense, readying ourselves for death is really an ever-widening entry into life.

John Powell, in his book *Unconditional Love,* tells the story of a young student of his who was dying of cancer. In the final stages of his illness, he came to see Powell and said something to this effect: "Father, you once told us something in class that has made it easier for me to die young. You said: 'There are only two potential tragedies in life, and dying young isn't one of them. These are the two real tragedies: *If you go through life and you don't love . . . and if you go through life and you don't tell those whom you love that you love them.*' When the doctors told me that I didn't have very long to live, I realized how much I have been loved. I've been able to tell my family and others how much they mean to me. I've expressed love. People ask me: 'What's it like being twenty-four years old and dying?' I tell them: 'It's not so bad. It beats being fifty years old and having no values!'"

For Powell, we prepare ourselves for death by loving deeply and especially by expressing love, appreciation, and gratitude to each other. Jesus says much the same thing. When the woman at Bethany poured an entire bottle of expensive ointment on his feet and dried his feet with her hair, he commented on her lavish expression of affection and gratitude by saying: "She has just anointed me for my impending death." What he meant by that should not be piously misinterpreted. He wasn't saying: "Since I am going to be dead in a while anyway, let her waste this ointment!" He was saying rather: "When I come to die, it is going to be easier because, at this moment, I am truly tasting life! It's easier to die when one has been, even for a moment, fully alive."

I think that had the old monk cornered Jesus and asked him the question he asked me, he might have heard something like the following: "Prepare for death by living more fully, work at loving more deeply, less discriminately, more affectionately, and more gratefully. Tell someone close to you today that you love him or her."

EVER SO BRIEF A GLORY

The last couple of years have not been particularly kind to my family. Two years ago, a sister was lost to cancer; this spring, a brother-in-law died suddenly of a heart attack while at work; right now, we wait and pray as another sister is dying of cancer. In each case, death has claimed a young person, someone still in the bloom of life.

Our family has faith. In the end, we believe that resurrection will bring us all together again, and that ultimately, in the words of Julian of Norwich, "all will be well, and all will be well, and every manner of being will be well." There will be celebrations still in the future — with everyone there. Of that we should have no doubt.

But that future can seem a long way off, and belief in resurrection in some indefinite future offers scant consolation in the definite present. So we grasp for some seeds of consolation in the present, something to hang on to, as we face losing yet another young member of our family.

Dying young is a compound tragedy. There is the loss of a life, a goodbye with a finality that cauterizes the heart. Nobody and nothing can prepare you for the reality of death, the finality, the irrevocability, the severance. Death has a sting, a whopping one, despite Christian faith. This is true of every death. When someone dies young the tragedy doubles.

Life is cut off in bloom and there is a sickening waste of health, of beauty, of love, of opportunity.

Few things scar the heart as badly as the sight of the premature erosion of beauty and the untimely corruption of flesh. When you see the taut flesh of freshness and young life give way to the slack, sickly odor of death, there is no mercy on the heart. First it posits anger. Bitterness can easily follow.

But even without anger, it still posits the question: Why? Why all this for so short a time? Why an ending when so much is just beginning? Why all these years of effort, growth, learning, loving, maturing, to be cut off just at bloom? Why a parent dying, a spouse dying, a loving nun dying, when they are still so badly needed — not to mention wanted?

I was sitting in my office last night luxuriating in self-pity when some small seed of consolation dropped right at my feet, literally. For a reason that may seem slightly sadistic, I always keep a hibiscus plant in my room. The reason is because one of the features of that plant is that it rarely blooms, though it does so in spectacular color. Its flowers last exactly twenty-four hours — and perhaps nobody even sees them. Yet nature makes no apologies for this, and everything about it assures us that the whole thing is worthwhile.

Last night a hibiscus bloom, unusually beautiful and just one day old and already withered, dropped at my foot. That too posits something. A bloom, however beautiful, is only for a very short while, and sometimes nobody even sees it. Nature works like that.

Life is nature and nature is life. So life is brief and the power and health and beauty of our bodies bloom ever so briefly and often go mostly unnoticed. That is also true for all that we give bloom to, our human loves, our infatuations, our honeymoons, our achievements, our securities. It's all hibiscus flower — beautiful, so much work and nature and feeling constellated in a spectacular bloom that's destined to begin to die just as it reaches full flower.

Yet, nothing is lost in nature. Each flower changes the world and no sparrow falls from the sky, save God notices and marks the event in the great eternal book from which, some day, all that is hidden will be revealed.

Without every sparrow that's ever flown and without every hibiscus flower that ever gave up its life on the day of its birth, the world would be slightly different. And that exceptionally beautiful hibiscus bloom, with its ever so brief glory, reminds us that a day of bloom is infinitely better than an eternity of plastic. And so beautiful flowers wither and die and we look on and we cry, but with real tears, spilt over real life and real beauty.

DYING FROM
A TERMINAL ILLNESS

Have you ever stood by the bed of someone dying of a terminal disease or of old age and, in pain and anger, wondered why death sometimes works the way it does? Often the question is not only, Why does this person have to die? Rather, the harder question is: Why does this person have to die like this? Why does that person have to be so humiliated, suffer such great pain, be unable to do even the most basic things for himself or herself, and be reduced to an infantile helplessness — but without the freshness, attractiveness, and healthy bodily smells of a baby? Why is death so often shrouded in pain, humiliation, helplessness, and groaning?

Death is partly mystery, and so there can be no full answer to these questions. Yet faith, and experience, can help us somewhat. Allow me to share a personal story:

Recently I watched my own sister die of cancer. From the

time she was first diagnosed until she died almost exactly five years later, the cancer did its slow deadly work. Beyond the ravages of the disease itself there were operations that mutilated her body and treatments that sapped her energy and slowly killed her mind and spirit as well. We, her family, and many others too who loved her stood around helplessly, frustrated, offering what scant support and consolation we could. Finally, in the last weeks, the disease and the drugs needed to kill the pain took over completely and she was reduced to a shell of her former self, utterly helpless, unable to take care of even her most elementary bodily needs, unable even to speak.

She was literally reduced to a baby, not just in her own helplessness but also in the way we all, inadvertently, treated her — feeding her as we would a baby, speaking condescendingly to her as we would to a child, and trying to coax a smile or a laugh out of her and then congratulating her and ourselves when we succeeded. And, all this time, she was sinking ever more deeply into a pain that even the strongest drugs could no longer make bearable.

Watching all of this, at one stage, all of us around her began to feel both bewildered and angry. Why? Why is an adult, a beautiful healthy woman, reduced to this? Why such helplessness and humiliation, not to mention pain? A baby, at least, in such helplessness speaks of development and the baby's very smells are healthy. An adult, in such a state, speaks only of disease and disintegration.

But at a point there was also a partial answer, one that surprised us and that came from her pain and humiliation. Someone had just coaxed a timid smile out of her, and we were struck at how much like a baby she had become. In my own anger at this, I suddenly realized something: *she was about to be reborn. How fitting that she should again be a baby!*

The image fits, except for one thing, her great pain. Why such pain in a baby that is about to be born?

Then something else became clear: dying like this, *she was both baby and mother.* Her groans were those of a mother in labor. She was both giving birth and being born. This latter element, of partially being mother in her own birth, was even more strongly borne out during the last twenty hours before she died. During those hours she went into a coma. She withdrew from us and was engaged in some struggle that was now more private and more extreme. Her breathing became very heavy and labored and she literally groaned and moaned as she struggled to let go, to give birth, and to be born all at the same time. At this point, none of us present thought any more of her helplessness, her lost health, her lost beauty, her humiliation, nor, indeed, even very much about her pain and impending death. We could only think of labor pains, her struggle to give birth even as she herself was the child about to be born.

After the birth of a child I have often heard talk of the mother being in labor for a number of hours — "she was in labor for fourteen hours!" Having never actually witnessed a birth, I have not been clear as to exactly what that meant. I think, now, that I have some idea. My sister was in labor for twenty hours before she gave herself (and was given) final birth. Some women friends of mine have also shared with me that, when they were giving birth, they were in excruciating pain right up to the second of birth. Immediately afterward there was a certain ecstasy. I can only imagine and suggest that this is also what happened to my sister when she died . . . and is what happens to millions and millions of others who suffer and die in this way.

TERMINAL ILLNESS AS
THE PASSION OF CHRIST

Something else was evident in the death of my sister — something which is perhaps the least understood aspect in the way that Christ died and in the way many persons who die from terminal illnesses parallel that death. When we look at Christ's life and death we see a curious design: *a long period of intense activity, within which he is the one who is giving and doing, is followed by a brief period before his death within which he is helpless, passive, and is the one to whom things are being given and done to.* From the time he begins his public ministry until the night before his death, for the most part, he is the active one. He is the one who teaches, heals, feeds, consoles, challenges, and prays for others. He is the doer — the miracle worker, the community-builder, the instituter of cult, the minister. Only to a lesser degree do others minister to him. Then, from the time he is arrested in the garden until he dies, things reverse. He enters his passion (passiveness/*passio*); his ministry now is to be receptive, passive, to let others do things to him. During his final hours, he does nothing except submit to what is being done to him.

It is both curious and ironic that it was precisely in those last painful hours, when he was most passive in terms of activity and ministry, that Christ did the most for us in terms of salvation. We were graced through what Christ did for us during his active ministry, but we are particularly saved through what he did for us in his passion and death, a time when, in our ordinary manner of perception, he appears least active and most helpless in terms of doing anything for us.

My sister's life and death closely parallel this design. Like Christ, she died young. Cancer caught her in the prime of her life and she died just days after her fifty-fourth birthday.

During her whole adult life she had distinguished herself as the prototype *doer*, homemaker, teacher, and, for the last sixteen years of her life, dean of students at an all-girls academy where she was mother, big sister, nun, counselor, doctor, advocate, and companion to hundreds of young women. She also played the same role in our own family, replacing my parents after they died twenty years ago and being, for the rest of us, the family center and organizer. And she loved it, she loved being the doer!

But, like Christ too, in the last days of her life the roles reversed. She was passive, the one to whom things were being done, and, like Christ too, I don't doubt for one minute that she was able to do more for us and give more to us during her passion than during all those years when she actively did so much for us. In a fine little book entitled *In Memoriam*, Henri Nouwen describes his own mother's death. He tells how painful and great was her struggle to accept death fully in faith, to let go, and how this so shattered his own previous naive fantasy of how a woman so full of goodness and faith should ideally die. For a time, he admits, it did not make sense, until he realized how closely her death paralleled Christ's. She had Christ's selflessness, his heart and mind; should it not make sense, he hints, that she die like him?

Why is the death of good people so often shrouded in pain, humiliation, struggle, helplessness, and groaning? Because, as can be seen in Christ's death (and in my sister's death and in the death of millions of others), there is birth within death, death within birth, receiving within giving, giving within receiving. The mystery of redemption, as can be seen from Christ's life and death, is deep, paradoxical, partly unfathomable, constantly surprising, and always life-giving.

DEATH, A SECOND BIRTH

Carlo Carretto once said that nothing is more evident than the existence of God — and nothing is more obscure. That is also true of life after death. As Christians we believe that death is really a birth to a new and fuller life. But that is not easy to believe.

We are sensual creatures, in every meaning of that phrase. That is our nature. We draw life through our senses and we believe in what we can see, feel, touch, taste, smell, and picture on the basis of imaginative constructs based upon those senses. And so it is hard to imagine, let alone believe in, a world totally beyond this present one. Our imaginations simply run dry. Dust thou art and unto dust thou shalt return: that is imaginable. Less imaginable is that beyond the dust of our present lives lies life in a world radically different from the one we know here and that death is really a birth into that world. It is hard to imagine "the resurrection of the body and life everlasting."

Imaginable or not, that is what our faith asks us to do. To be a Christian, especially as regards belief in life after death, is precisely to open our imaginations to the unimaginable, our minds to the nonconceptual, and our hearts to the holy.

Imagine that you could talk to a baby in the womb before it was born. Having never seen the light of this world, knowing only the confines and securities of the womb, the baby would, I suspect, be pretty skeptical about your story of the existence of a world beyond the womb. You would be hard pushed to convince it to believe both that outside of its mother's womb there exists a world infinitely larger than what it is presently experiencing and that it is to its advantage to eventually be born into that immense world. On the basis of its experience, the baby simply would lack the tools to imagine the world that you are talking about. Unable to picture the world you are describing, it would have difficulty in believing in it and letting go of the world it knows, the womb, to want to be born. If a baby in the womb were conscious, it would have to make a real act of faith to believe in life after birth. It would fear birth as much as most of us fear death.

When we fear death we are, in terms of the bigger picture given us by faith, precisely babies in the womb fearing birth. This world, for all its immensity and for all it offers, is simply another womb, bigger, to be sure, than our mother's womb, but ultimately rather small and constricting in terms of full and eternal life. And, like babies in the womb, we find it virtually impossible to imagine life beyond our present experience. Thus, we cling to what we know, to what gives us life, the umbilical cord, and fear anything and everything that might loosen our grip on that. We fear life after death in the same way as a baby fears life after birth.

But life after birth has the identical dynamics of life in the womb. We are still being gestated, save that now we call it aging, and inevitable is the day when a new pelvic thrust, death, will awaken, in deep inchoate recesses of our minds and bodies, the memory of just such a push many years earlier. Again, as years earlier, a glaring passage of light will promise a new world and, again, we will not have much say in the matter of birth. We will have to trust that being born is what is best for us.

To my mind, there are few things as helpful in understanding death as is the analogy of birth, except that it is, in the end, not an analogy. Death, seen through the eyes of faith, is not like a birth; it is a birth. We are initially born from our mothers' wombs into a very large world, one which, for quite a period of time, leaves us literally speechless. However, this seemingly immense world is ultimately just another womb within which we are again being gestated and readied for birth into a yet larger world which, I suspect, will in its magnitude and beauty stun us into a new speechlessness.

Moreover, just as initially we had to first be born before we could see our mothers, even though they were carrying us in their wombs, so now we must first die, be born again, before we can see our true mother, God. Then too, after this second birth, just as after the first, we will lie open-mouthed and awestruck before a beauty, magnitude, and love that we could not have hoped to ever imagine. Birth and death require the same act of faith, the trust that a fuller life and a more meaningful contact with the mother awaits us beyond this present womb.

LOVE IS RESILIENT

We know that Christ has risen from the dead because, despite all death and wounds, love exists and love continues in the world. Charity is the new life of Easter.

Recently I was at a conference given by Maya Angelou. She is the black American poet who spoke at Bill Clinton's inauguration. Among other things, she told the story of her childhood. When she was seven years old, one night she was raped by a neighbor. She told her grandmother, who called the police. Her assailant was arrested and put in prison. Criminals within prisons have their own codes and one of them is that sex offenders are themselves often tortured and killed by fellow inmates. This was the case for her attacker. Soon after his arrest he was murdered by his fellow prisoners. Her seven-year-old mind and heart, already severely traumatized by the rape, was not able to deal with this. Quite naturally, she blamed herself. The effect of this was so severe that for nearly ten years she was unable to speak. She was put into special schools, seen as handicapped, retarded, abnormal, and this wreaked great psychological and social havoc. It is hard to imagine a more wounded and broken childhood than hers.

But she has recovered, learned to speak again, and eventually has become a gifted speaker, opera singer, writer, and poet. More importantly, she has become a woman of rare vibrancy, zest, graciousness, style, warmth, gratefulness, faith, and love — complete with an exceptional sense of humor and delight. As we look at and listen to the Maya Angelou of today, it borders on the impossible to believe she is the same person who endured her own childhood. When she speaks she tells you her secret: faith. But hers is a particular kind of faith, a faith in the resurrection. She has her own, one-line wording for this: resiliency is the key to love.

Listening to her, I was reminded of a song I heard years ago, a Civil War song called, "The Night They Drove Old Dixie Down." The singer is telling the story of her brother, killed in the war. It is a beautiful song, expressing a deep melancholy that is full of a noble stoicism, but contains no hope. Her young brother is dead, killed senselessly in war:

> He was just eighteen
> Proud and brave
> When a Yankee laid him in his grave.
> I swear by the mud below my feet
> You can't raise a Caine back up
> When it's in defeat.

Listening to Maya Angelou's story helped awaken in us, her listeners, the central tenet of our faith: you can raise life back up when it's in defeat! There is resurrection, and this puts all wound and death into a completely different focus. It also calls on us to move beyond our wounds and our deaths. Resiliency is the key to love.

Stories like Maya Angelou's are proof of the resurrection, proof that the grave of Christ was empty, proof that love is more resilient than the many things that crucify it. Love and laughter go on. Charity is the new life of Easter. I believe that Jesus was resurrected from the dead because of the many Maya Angelous that I have met. I have experienced charity, love, forgiveness, and resiliency. I have seen the new life of Easter. In Maya's story, and in our own stories, we see that dead bodies do rise from their graves, that dead voices do sing again, that abused bodies do delight again in joy, and that wounded spirits do grow strong again and forgive.

This is the challenge of Easter, the challenge of the resurrection. It invites us to new life, charity, and resiliency. Faith in the resurrection is the only thing that can ultimately empower us to live beyond our own crucifixions, beyond being raped, beyond being muted by wound.

A friend of mine once sent me an Easter card that ended with the challenge: may you leave behind you a string of empty tombs! Let our wounded, muted voices begin to sing again: Christ is risen! Life is very, very good!

THE COMMUNION OF SAINTS

I believe in the communion of saints! This is a dogma of our creed upon which we too seldom reflect. What does it mean to believe in a communion of saints? Simply stated, it means that, as Christians, we believe that we are still in communion with those who have died. Among other things, this says that we can relate to them, speak to them, and be spoken to by them. The bond of love and of family still exists between those who have died and ourselves, and we can still be present to each other and influence each other's lives.

That sounds like wishful thinking. Wouldn't it be nice if that were true! Well, it is true. It's an article of faith. Sadly, today, we rarely live our lives in face of that, and we are the poorer for it. There is a rich mysticism, not to mention an immense fountain of grace and consolation, lying untapped here. Allow me to illustrate with just one example.

Last winter, I attended a large religious education conference in Los Angeles. Its theme was the resurrection, its logo was the rainbow, and its closing liturgy brought together about six thousand people. At that eucharist, after communion, when all the hymns had been sung and everything was quiet, a young couple walked up to the altar and picked up the microphone. They looked up at the more than six thousand who were gathered there and shared their story.

About a year before, their twelve-year-old son had died of cancer. He had died after a long struggle. They were, naturally, devastated. Nothing prepares parents for the death of a child, and nothing, on this side of eternity, can soften its blow. Nature itself is set up in reverse: children are equipped to bury their parents, tough as that is, but not the other way around. Children are meant to outlive their parents.

The morning after their son's death they were sitting with friends in the living room of their home, drinking coffee and attempting to console each other, when their phone rang. It was a neighbor. "Quickly, go look out of your front door!" he exhorted. "You'll see something unique."

They rushed to look and there, before them, was a rainbow the like of which they had never seen before, in terms of its spectacular color as well as its scope (it extended perfectly without flaw from the edge of one horizon to the edge of the other). They were, of course, taken by its beauty and by its symbolism (rainbows are a symbol of hope, God's promise, and the resurrection), but they were even more taken by the clear, unmistakable intuition that it was their son who was doing these particular fireworks for their benefit. As they watched in awe, and in faith, the mother heard her son say to her gently: "Mum, this is for you! And because it is hard for you to believe it, I will do it again, the same way, for you tomorrow at this same time!"

All doubts that they had, thoughts that this was some trick of their imaginations or mere wishful thinking induced by fatigue, sorrow, and longing, were erased the next day when, at exactly the same time, the identical rainbow reappeared. Their son was speaking to them and they, I am sure, will now forever know what it means to believe in the communion of saints.

I believe their story, not just because they appeared to be very sane and balanced persons, nor because they had enough nerve to share this in front of thousands of people, but because what they shared is not something weird, exotic, new age, or even all that extraordinary. The story they shared is what the dogma of the communion of saints means when it is taken out of the credal formulae, out of the theology texts, and out of the realm of the abstract, and put into our lives.

There is a rich mysticism here, a rich grace, a deep consolation. We must take this item of our creed far more seriously. Christian tradition puts it into a dogma and that tradition, as G. K. Chesterton once suggested, "may be defined as an extension of the franchise. Tradition means giving votes to the most obscure of all classes, the dead. It is the democracy of the dead. It refuses to submit to the small and arrogant oligarchy of those who merely happen to be walking around. All democrats object to persons being disqualified by the accident of birth; [Christian] tradition objects to their being disqualified by the accident of death" (*Orthodoxy*, 83).

Chapter 7

Walking Justly and Not Just Piously

The Call to Social Justice

THE NOBODIES

We are not, but could be.
We don't speak languages, but dialects.
We don't have religions, but superstitions.
We don't create art, but handicrafts.
We don't have culture, but folklore.
We are not human beings, but human resources.
We do not have faces, but arms.
We do not have names, but numbers.
We do not appear in the history of the world,
   but in the police blotter of the local papers.
The nobodies, who are not worth
   the bullets that kill them.
     — EDUARDO GALEANO, *The Book of Embraces*

THE SEVEN SOCIAL SINS

    Politics without principle
    Wealth without work
    Commerce without morality
    Pleasure without conscience
    Education without character
    Science without humanity
    Worship without sacrifice
      — MOHANDAS K. GANDHI

SOCIAL JUSTICE —
NEW KNOWLEDGE/NEW RESPONSIBILITY

Former Jesuit superior general Pedro Arrupe was once asked why there is such an emphasis today on social justice when, in the past, many saintly persons and good spiritual writings appeared almost entirely to neglect this, at least in terms of an explicit development. He answered rather simply: "Today we know more!"

He is right. In the past, because we knew less, it was possible to be good and saintly and less involved in social justice, despite the fact that Scripture and Christ's explicit teaching make the call to justice just as nonnegotiable as the call to prayer and private morality. Today we know more, not just because modern communications daily show us the victims of injustice on our television screens and in our newspapers, but also, and especially, because we are less sociologically naive. Put positively, this lack of naivete means that we understand better how social systems affect us, both for good and for bad — and social justice is really about how *systems* affect us, especially adversely.

It is very important that this be understood. Although they interpenetrate each other and depend upon each other, social justice and social morality are distinct from private charity and private morality. Private morality is something that I do on my own. Other persons might guide me or inspire me, but, in the end, I am moral and charitable on the basis of my own personal goodness and personal actions. Social justice, on the other hand, has to do with the social systems I am part of and participate in. I can be a good person in my private life, churchgoing, prayerful, kind, honest, gentle, and generous in my dealings with others, and still, at the same time, be part of a social, economic, political, and even ecclesial system that is unfair in that it works for the benefit of some at the cost of victimizing others. Issues such as war, poverty, violation of the ecology, feminism, native rights, abortion, and racism (to name just a few) are caused not simply, nor indeed any longer *primarily,* by individual persons acting in bad conscience and doing bad things, but by huge impersonal systems that are inherently unfair and are, to an extent, beyond the control of the individuals who participate in them.

Let me try to illustrate the difference between social justice and private charity with a story, famous in social justice circles:

> Once upon a time there was a town which was built beyond the bend in a river. One day some of its children were playing by the river when they spotted three bodies floating in the water. They ran to get help and the townsfolk quickly pulled the bodies from the river. One body was dead so they buried it. One was alive, but quite ill, so they put it into the hospital. The third was a healthy child, so they placed it in a family who cared for it and took it to school. From that day on, each day a number of bodies came floating around the bend in the river and, each day, the good charitable townspeople pulled them out and tended to them — burying the dead, caring for the sick, finding homes for the children, and so on. This went on for years, and the townspeople came to expect that each day would bring its quota of bodies. But, during those years, nobody thought to walk up the river, beyond the bend, and check out why, daily, those bodies came floating down the river.

The difference between private charity and social justice is, in one way, the difference between handling the bod-

ies that have come down the river and doing preventive
work up the river. It is more complex than that, especially
when one sees the web of intertwined social, political, historical, and economic factors responsible for those bodies,
but the analogy at least helps show a key distinction. Private
morality has more to do with personal charity and personal
goodness and honesty. Social justice has to do more with
changing systems which, although often managed by persons in good conscience, are of themselves evil in that they,
knowingly or unknowingly, victimize certain people. Thus,
for instance, a person may be very sincere and, in private
life, very charitable, gentle, prayerful, and moral. Yet that
person might, blindly, unknowingly (through work, political
affiliations, economic ideology and investments, and simply
by a consumeristic lifestyle), participate in and help sustain
systems which are far from charitable, gentle, prayerful, and
moral. What's good for that person might be horrible for
others.

When Pedro Arrupe said, "Today we know more!" he was
referring precisely to the fact that current sociological and
economic analysis has shown us, with clarity, how our political, economic, social, and ecclesial systems, irrespective of
how individually sincere we might be in our support of them,
are unfair and wounding to so many others. Given this, our ignorance is less inculpable and the imperative to "walk justly"
becomes less escapable.

WAGING PEACE

Recently a young high school student wrote a letter to the
editorial section of our local city paper. In her youthful idealism, she was profoundly disappointed that we, as a country
(Canada), cannot come to an agreement on a new consti-

tution and are in danger of breaking up. Her comment was most interesting. She didn't, as do most, simplistically blame the politicians: "How can we keep this country together if we have incompetent politicians? What can we, good people, do when we are led by bad leaders?" She suggested something else: "I suspect that we will never agree on anything in this country, but what can you expect in a nation of pampered people!"

Her comment puts a finger on one of the major reasons why so much of our peacemaking is ineffectual, despite our sincere intentions and efforts. We are too blind to the fact that the greed, the wars, and the violence that we see being played out on a world stage (and that we blame politicians and world leaders for) are, to a large extent, merely a magnification of what is happening inside our own hearts and among us in our private relationships. When we watch the news at night, most of what we are seeing is a reflection of what is inside ourselves.

Today almost all groups that work for peace, both liberal and conservative, do not take this seriously enough. There is an intrinsic, never-to-be-neglected connection between what seems radically private and what is political and social. Thus there can be no peace on the big stage when there is greed, jealousy, unwillingness to forgive, and unwillingness to compromise within our private hearts. When the outer body gets sick, it nearly always signals a breakdown in the internal immune system. Hence, given the state of our world today, one can be pretty sure that there is not much in the way of antibodies (charity, joy, peace, patience, goodness, long-suffering, faith, mildness, gentleness, and chastity) within the body of humanity, namely, within our private lives.

When we cannot get along with each other within our own marriages and families, we should not be surprised that countries do not get along with each other. When we cannot move beyond past hurts in our own lives, we should not expect the issues causing violence in Northern Ireland, Israel, Bosnia, Iran, and the Sudan to be resolved by better politics. When we spend billions of dollars a year on cosmetics and clothing that serve to build up our appearance so as to be less vulnerable, we have no right to self-righteously demand that governments cut their budgets for defense. Finally, when nearly all of us have borrowed money so as to have, right now, the things we cannot yet afford but want, then we should have some understanding of why our countries have all overspent and are hopelessly in debt.

There are many aspects to waging peace. The social justice literature of the past decades has given us a crucial insight which should never again be lost, namely, that private virtue and private charity alone are not enough. There is sociology as well as psychology, systemic evil as well as private sin. In the face of unjust systems and corrupt governments, Christians cannot get away with simply practicing private virtue and saying to their less fortunate neighbors: "I wish you well. (Stay warm and well-fed!) I'm a good and honest person. I did nothing to cause your suffering!" There are real social and political issues underlying war, poverty, oppression, and violence. Peacemaking must address these.

But there are real private, personal issues as well. Hence, waging peace requires more than simply confronting the powers that be. What must, ultimately, be confronted is our own greed, our own hurt, our own jealousy, our own inability to forgive, compromise, and respect. More than we need to convert bad systems, we need to convert ourselves. We, in the Western world at least, are not a bunch of good, generous, forgiving people who have the misfortune of being governed by a small group of bad and selfish individuals who in no way reflect us.

There is a story told about a Lutheran pastor, a Norwegian, who was arrested by the Gestapo during the Second World War. When he was brought into the interrogation room, the Gestapo officer placed his revolver on the table between them and said: "Father, this is just to let you know that we are serious!" The pastor, instinctively, pulled out his Bible and laid it beside the revolver. The officer demanded: "Why did you do that?" The pastor replied: "You laid out your weapon — and so did I!"

In waging peace we must keep in mind what our true weapons are and who the real enemy is.

TENDERNESS AND POLITICS

Few things are as singularly urgent as is the need to bring about a better marriage between contemplation and justice. The tension that exists between them expresses itself in a variety of ways. It is the perennial tension between piety and politics, private morality and social engagement, biblical righteousness and social justice, your local prayer group and Greenpeace, tenderness and hard action. Ernst Käsemann once put it simply. The trouble in the world and in the church, he suggested, is that the pious are not liberal and the liberal are not pious.

Few people resolve this tension very well. Invariably we fall off one side or the other: When worship, piety, and private morality are the dominant focus of our religious lives, we too often tend to rationalize away the gospel's demand for social justice. Religion then means going to church, praying privately, and keeping our private morals roughly in order. In circles of piety frequently there is little sense that true worship of God demands more than churchgoing and private morality.

Conversely, when social justice is the dominant focus of our religious lives, we too easily confuse Greenpeace with the gospel and forget that what ultimately grounds our commitment to justice is Jesus Christ, not liberal ideology. In social justice circles there is often too little sense that the commitment to justice demands more than merely having a just cause and doing effective political action.

One person who, to my mind, has found a rare balance here and who serves both as a challenge and a model for the rest of us is Jim Wallis, the founder of the Sojourners community in Washington, D.C. Wallis and his Sojourners community are in the front lines in virtually every justice issue in America; they are also a community on the front lines of Christian worship and private morality. And they are not a Johnny-come-lately to either of these. Right from its inception Sojourners, mainly through the vision and articulation of Wallis, committed itself nonnegotiably to both personal righteousness and social justice, private morality and social transformation, piety and liberality. They married these, the church and the street, in a way that very few others have.

The years have not been kind to that marriage, just as they haven't been to most marriages. Pressures of all kinds, from the right and from the left, tempt them, and everyone else, to give up on that marriage. But, fortunately, the reverse seems to be happening. What is coming out of Sojourners, as seen both in the literature it is producing and in the social actions it is taking, is a model for how contemplation and justice, private and social morality should meet. In Sojourners we see a paradigm for how the church and the street, piety and politics, might mix, namely, in a gospel that is not divided, but that embraces both the call to conversion and the summons to justice, a gospel that integrates prayer, worship, private morality, and social transformation.

> The frightening disregard for human life among too many young people is a bitter reflection on the way these same young people have become so utterly disregarded by their society. The coldness of heart that makes even veteran urban activists shiver is a judgment upon our coldness toward our poorest children. We reap what we have sown.
>
> Neither liberal sociology nor conservative piety can begin to address the roots of this crisis. Neither government spending nor simplistic self-help slogans will suffice. What is called for now is that particular biblical combination of which the prophets most often spoke — *justice and righteousness.* Both the structures of oppression and the morality of personal behavior must undergo radical transformation. We need a change of heart and a change of direction not only among troubled urban youth, but for all of us.
>
> The problem is too deep and our task too large to take it on by ourselves. We will need the help that comes "by faith." As another young man in the post-riot meeting in Watts said to us: "We've got some habits that only God can cure." That goes for all of us. ("Worth Fighting For," *Sojourners*, February–March 1994)

Wallis goes on to suggest that at this critical historical juncture only faith will make possible the political imagination needed to find solutions to the social problems that beset us. He sees signs of hope already emerging. He is one of them!

SOCIAL JUSTICE REVISITED

Few groups have acted with as much moral passion and energy during these past years as have the various social justice
groups within the church and within society. From church
basements, from the offices of Greenpeace, from feminist
circles, from anti-war protesters, from pro-life and pro-choice
rallies, and from many other places, there has issued forth a
moral energy and challenge that few can be deaf to or can
choose to ignore.

But ... there has been more energy than impact. Save for a
few salient exceptions having to do with racism and feminism,
the mainstream culture has been able to marginalize both the
groups and their concerns. This would not be a cause for concern, given that the prophetic message is always marginalized
and "the world" is habitually opposed to Christ, except that,
in this case, too many people of good conscience find themselves able to write off most of the concerns of social justice
groups. Why is this? Why after more than twenty-five years of
such effort has social justice, for the main part, been unable
to crack mainstream conscience? Why, after all this effort,
are we unable oftentimes even to crack the conscience of
our own families?

The simplistic answer of course is that mainstream culture
and conscience are simply insincere, greedy, hard of heart,
and too caught up with their own selfish concerns to be open
to prophetic challenge. While there is some truth in that,
this answer is far from the whole truth. The whole truth is
that social justice action in both church and civic circles,
with hardly an exception, has been perennially plagued and
depotentiated by its own inherent flaws. Social justice has
not gone mainstream because, too often, even while it contained the truth, it undercut its own credibility. Why do I

say this? I can do little more than name some of the major reasons here.

- *The failure of social justice action to center itself in some-thing beyond the ideology of either the left or the right and to cloak itself in charity.* Far too often the challenge that is presented is not grounded so much in the gospel or in charity as it is in liberal or conservative criticism. What is at stake then is not so much justice or Christ's option for the poor as somebody's ideology. People can, in clear conscience, walk away from this.

- *The failure of social justice action to be healthily self-critical, to check its own strident voices, and to make judgments be-yond ideological black and white.* Until we as social justice advocates are able, when it is proper, to criticize our own, to check strident voices within our own ranks, to stop being ideologically simplistic in our judgments about who is right and who is wrong, and until we be-come less predictable in our rhetoric and indignations, we will never capture the mainstream conscience.

- *The failure of social justice action to be realistic in propos-ing justice and eco-ethics.* During the Gulf War the failure of many of the anti-war protesters to take seriously the evil of Saddam Hussein did a lot to make the warmakers themselves look like heros of conscience. The failure of many persons who are militantly defending the environ-ment to take seriously enough the four billion people on this planet who also need to live is a major reason why we do not yet have an eco-ethics that governments will actually buy into. The failure of many of us who preach social justice to take seriously enough the tyranny of affluence against which most people in the First World find themselves helpless is no small factor in helping maintain the status quo. When the challenge to justice is not realistic enough, mainstream conscience can, in good conscience, ignore it.

- *The failure of social justice action to resist the temptation to be selective regarding justice issues, our failure to truly present "an ethical seamless garment."* When people fighting for certain rights refuse, at the same time, to take other rights seriously, then good conscience will be divided from good conscience — as we see, for example, in the abortion debate where two justice issues are pitted against each other.

- *The failure to take seriously contemplation, aesthetics, and joy.* Doris Lessing once said that she left the Communist Party because it didn't believe in color. That speaks volumes and is a commentary on the drabness, colorlessness, oversensitivity, and simple heaviness that too often surrounds social justice circles. Small wonder we can be so easily written off!

UNNOTICED BLOOD

Over one hundred years ago as Therese of Lisieux lay dying she told her sister Pauline that the entire foundation of her spirituality came from her contemplation of the face of the suffering Christ ("the Holy Face," she called it). She described to her sister how she was always struck by the Good Friday texts (from Isaiah and from the gospels) that describe the face of God's suffering servant on earth, how that face is marred, unattractive, and either ignored or despised by those who see it.

Therese (whose real religious name, incidentally, was "Sister Therese *of the Holy Face*," and not "the little flower" or

"Therese of the Child Jesus") then tells Pauline: "One Sunday, looking at a picture of Our Lord on the Cross, I was struck by the blood flowing from one of his divine hands. I felt a pang of great sorrow when thinking this blood was falling to the ground without anyone's hastening to gather it up. I was resolved to remain in spirit at the foot of the Cross and to receive its dew" (*Story of a Soul*, 99). In a later conversation, she adds: "I don't want this precious blood to be lost. I shall spend my life gathering it up for the good of souls . . . for to live from love is to dry Your Face — *vivre d'amour c'est essuyer ta Face*" (*Last Conversations*, 126, 134).

This metaphor — noticing the preciousness of Christ's blood, gathering it up, and gently drying the face of the suffering Christ — is the metaphor Therese uses to describe her entire vocation. It is this which constitutes the deep foundation upon which she grounds the other elements of her spirituality.

For her, Christ is still bleeding in the sufferings of persons on this earth, in our sufferings, yours and mine. And, as was the case with Jesus, this blood is, mostly, dripping unnoticed, unvalued, and often to the tune of another's indifference and ridicule. Therese's sensitivity (which was born out of her own suffering, her deep prayer, and the unique way she was loved and valued and made to feel precious as a small child) alerted her to preciousness that was seemingly being wasted. The sight tore at her heart as if she were a sensitive artist watching a masterpiece being heartlessly defaced and destroyed; it so baptized and displaced her that her whole life became nothing else than an attempt to do something about it.

Before dying, Therese promised that she would even spend her eternity, heaven, coming back to earth to continue to gather these unnoticed drops of blood and to continue to dry the sufferer's face.

What a powerful and fruitful image this could be for contemporary spirituality as we struggle to bring together the demands of piety and private morality with the demands of social justice and committed action in the world. Martyrs' blood is still flowing, Christ's blood is still flowing, the suffering servant of God is still being ridiculed on this earth — both in the poor of the world (the victims of injustice) and in the workplaces and homes of the not-so-poor.

Christ's suffering is still going on, the cost of living charity, joy, peace, justice, patience, mildness, and chastity is evident in faces everywhere. Tragically, we are not inundated with spiritual artists who notice that something precious beyond words is being defaced and destroyed. Nobody seems too bent on "hastening to gather up" that blood, nobody seems to notice how uniquely precious it is, and nobody seems to have the fully discriminating insight, Therese's insight, into Christ's suffering face.

If Christ's suffering face was truly understood we would see the coming together of private morality and social justice, of circles of piety and social action, for social justice circles would recognize the preciousness, importance, and utter non-negotiability of the tiniest private moral, psychological, or spiritual action, and circles of piety would begin, immediately, to make the preferential option for the poor since they would immediately see that in the lives of the poor something precious beyond words is being defaced and destroyed — and nobody is noticing or caring!

Beyond that, once we would start saying to each other, "to live from love is to dry your face," our habitual propensity for anger, self-pitying, self-righteousness, and giving up in despair would give way to a resurrection of charity, joy, peace, justice, patience, mildness, and chastity in our lives.

Why? Because the faith of Christ is always built upon the blood of the martyrs.

What is needed, both in social justice and piety circles, are more persons with the insight of Therese of Lisieux, more persons who notice where Christ's blood is being spilt today and who say: "I don't want this precious blood to be lost. I shall spend my life gathering it up."

WHAT IF?

What if we all were a bit more consistent? What if we all had wider loyalties? What if we all were much slower to say either/or? What if we all took to heart the idea that a little learning is a dangerous thing and that a little ideology is more dangerous still and went on to understand how destructive of hope are lives and values that are only half thought out? What if we all remembered that a heresy is a truth that is nine-tenths spoken?

What if the pious were more liberal and the liberal were more pious? What if those who are so involved in prayer groups and in the quest of the spiritual life were to become equally committed to social action? What if those who stand out for their social action were to become equally obsessed with private prayer and private morality? What if those who are so taken up with private sexual morality were to become as sensitive in the area of social justice? What if both the pious and the liberal were to become slightly less fanatic?

What if liberals were to become known as much for their humility, respect of others, and personal prudence as they are already known for their social concern? What if conservatives were to define family values so widely as to include the welfare of the poor and of all races? What if liberals were able to know where to draw some boundaries even as they challenge others beyond rigidity? What if conservatives were suddenly to push for a greater courage in risk and openness even as they defend the hard-won wisdom of tradition? What if both liberals and conservatives were able to do as Jesus did and reach into their sacks and bring out the old as well as the new?

What if pro-life groups were to become as known for their defense of the poor, ethnic minorities, the ecology, and the imprisoned as they are for their defense of the unborn? What if feminist groups were to champion, in the name of women, the most defenseless of all groups in the world, the unborn? What if both groups were to become renowned for their gentleness, their respect of others, and their willingness to sit down and calmly discuss anything?

What if both men and women would adopt an attitude of sympathy toward both sexes, recognizing as Virginia Woolf says, that "life, for both of us, is arduous, difficult, and a perpetual struggle"? What if both men and women were more tender?

What if the church began to challenge people to enjoy sex even as it teaches clearly the value of chastity? What if we, the adult children of the enlightenment, were to preach the value of chastity even as we work toward a healthy liberation from sexual repression? What if both, the church and the world, recognized the importance of what the other is saying regarding sexuality?

What if all those purists on spiritual quests, with question marks around their necks, were able to understand the importance of the ecclesial, the concrete historical community, and the singular importance of obedience/genuflection in the movement toward God? What if the churches were to become as renowned for their challenge to be free-thinking as they are for their challenge to obedience? What if both, the churches and the emerging nonecclesial spiritualities, were to be more self-effacing, less righteous, less judgmental of the other?

What if theologians were to become as renowned for their children's stories as they are for their hermeneutical works? What if those who believe that all truth can be communicated only in single syllables were to read the scriptural commentaries of Raymond Brown? What if liturgists were appreciated as much for their practical understanding as they are for their sense of the tradition and aesthetics? What if those who planned the liturgies in your own parish were as sensitive to shoddy aesthetics and to saccharine elements in contemporary language and music as they are to noninclusive language and to the phrase "saved a wretch like me"?

What if religious columnists were genuinely as interested in bringing God's consolation and challenge to the world as they are in their own reputations?

What if?

Well, if these things happened, the incarnation, like a bud long lying dormant in dry ground, would slowly break open and a new hope would begin slowly to flow over a depressed planet.

DAVID FACING GOLIATH

There is no substitute for imagination. Without good images for integrating experience, brute reality overpowers us and leaves us feeling depressed and helpless. Unless our symbols are working, we have little hope of turning fate to destiny.

This is especially true regarding how we, as Christians, stand before a world that is not much given to love, justice, tenderness, and prayer. Often, especially if you are a sensitive person, you will feel overwhelmed by the seeming hopelessness of it. What can you do? The powers of the world seem so huge and omnipresent while you are so small and limited.

When we feel depressed in this way, a helpful image is the picture of David standing before Goliath. It is the archetypal image of good standing before evil, justice standing before rape and pillage, sensitivity standing before brute impersonality, and tenderness and feeling standing before iron and concrete.

Two forces face each other in a struggle to decide life and death, and from every indication what is good, just, and tender is hopelessly overmatched.

So here is the image: at one point in its history, Israel, which here represents God's cause, is in battle against the Philistines who (as the very word "philistine" still connotes) represent brutality, lack of justice, lack of feeling, lack of goodness, and lack of God.

Their champion is a giant, Goliath, a brute of unparalleled strength who, in the image, has no feelings, no sensitivity, no goodness. He walks onto the battlefield clothed in iron, seemingly an inanimate force, sneering, arrogant, utterly disdainful of all opposition. Beside him stands his armor-bearer, also clothed in iron.

On the other side stands Israel, totally intimidated by this brute strength, knowing that among them there is nobody who can fight Goliath on his own terms.

So they change the terms. Instead of taking their strongest man, clothing him in iron, and sending him out against Goliath, they send a young boy, David, with no armor at all. He goes out barefoot, with only a slingshot, more a boy's plaything than a weapon of war. And he cuts a pathetic figure. David walks onto the battlefield the naive child, unsophisticated in war, a joke. That is how Goliath sees him. "Am I a dog, that you come out against me with sticks? You're not an opponent even worth fighting. You're a joke! Come over here and I will cut off your head and feed it to the birds!" Godless forces do not cower when truth marches out to do battle against them.

But we know the outcome. David reaches into his shepherd's pouch, takes out his slingshot, inserts a smooth pebble, and his first shot penetrates the skull of the giant. He then cuts off Goliath's head with his own sword. The boy fells the giant; the plaything of a child overpowers the weapons of war; the naive defeats the sophisticated and sensitivity proves more powerful than brute iron. There is a lesson to be gleaned from this.

That image, David before Goliath, the child before the giant, depicts how anyone who is a true defender of God's cause always stands before the world, hopelessly overmatched, naive, a child before an adult, bare skin against iron, a joke not to be taken seriously. But victory belongs to the child. It is the giant that is vulnerable; it is iron that falls, providing the child has a shepherd's pouch, a bag with smooth pebbles, and a plaything that the child has spent many hours palming and pressing.

What is the image here? What is the shepherd's pouch? What is the plaything? When David reached into his shepherd's pouch and took out a slingshot and a smooth pebble, you can be sure that this was not the first time he did this. As a shepherd, off in the fields by himself, he would have spent countless hours practicing with his slingshot, countless hours searching for smooth pebbles, and many more hours palming those pebbles to know their exact feel, to really make them his own. Long before we walk onto any battlefield to confront the giant, we too need to spend countless lonely hours palming and polishing what is in our shepherd's pouch: prayer, sacraments, our traditions.

These are David's pebbles, our weapons against Goliath. Through many lonely hours we need to palm them, press them, and give them the smell and feel of our own skin. Then, when we fling them at the giant, they will penetrate the iron and brute power that stand in the way of God. And even if we don't save the world, we will save our own sanity.

Chapter 8

Walking Honestly and Finding Our Souls among the Little Ones

The Call to Humility

"What is Real?" asked the Rabbit one day, when they were lying side by side near the nursery fender, before Nana came to tidy the room. "Does it mean having things that buzz inside you and a stickout handle?"

"Real isn't how you are made," said the Skin Horse. "It's a thing that happens to you. When a child loves you for a long, long time, not just to play with, but really loves you, then you become real."

"Does it hurt?" asked the Rabbit.

"Sometimes," said the Skin Horse, for he was always truthful, "When you are Real you don't mind being hurt."

"Does it happen all at once, like being wound up," he asked, "or bit by bit?"

"It doesn't happen all at once," said the Skin Horse. "You become. It takes a long time. That's why it doesn't often happen to people who break easily, or have sharp edges, or who have to be carefully kept. Generally, by the time you are Real, most of your hair has been loved off, and your eyes drop out and you get loose in the joints and very shabby. But these things don't matter at all, because once you are Real you can't be ugly, except to people who don't understand."   — Margery Williams, *The Velveteen Rabbit*

Lost is a place, too.

— Christina Crawford, *Survivor*

143

SIN BRAVELY

You are as sick as your sickest secret! That's a phrase some Alcoholics Anonymous groups use to challenge people to understand what, at its roots, sobriety really is. Drunkenness, of all kinds, has much more to do with lying than it has to do with alcohol, drugs, or anything else. We are sober, truly sober, when we stop lying.

I point this out because, today, everywhere, the prevailing temptation is to lie. Very little invites us to real honesty, to face our sickest secrets and make a searing act of contrition. Rationalization is more the rule and is, to my mind, perhaps the leading spiritual disease of our time. Everything conspires with us to bury our sickest secrets so deeply that, after a time, we are no longer even aware that they are there and to rationalize them so that, eventually, we don't even realize that they, and we, are sick. This is a dangerous game. The health of our souls is what is at stake here.

A few years ago, a twenty-six-year-old filmmaker made a movie which he intriguingly entitled *Sex, Lies, and Videotape*. It won first prize at the Cannes festival. At the risk of an irreverent comparison, this movie makes a good commentary on the ninth chapter of John's Gospel, where John uses his famous story of the man born blind to teach us a basic truth: We don't have to be sinless, bright, or even religiously interested to find Christ and, eventually, give ourselves over to him. We just have to be honest. We just have to stop lying!

Sex, Lies, and Videotape says much the same thing, save that it substitutes the concept of health for Christ. Its story line is quite simple. A young man, with every kind of dysfunction in his background and with a sick sexual neurosis, makes a vow that he will never again tell a lie. Whatever other sin or whatever other folly he might fall into because of weakness, circumstance, or hurt, he resolves that he will never again lie. And he invites others, in his own warped way, to follow him in this. So he sets up a cheap video camera and invites people to come and, with as much honesty as they can muster, speak into the camera and tell the story of their sexual lives. An interesting thing happens. All those who come and who speak honestly get better, grow gentler, and eventually get healthy, irrespective of whatever weaknesses and perversions they have. Conversely, all those who lie, who do not face the truth, slide ever deeper into hardness, rationalization, and self-deception. Maybe it's stretching things to say that when those people faced the camera and began to tell their sickest secrets we see the secular equivalent of the sacrament of confession, but it is a curious irony that many people who for all kinds of reasons regard sacramental reconciliation with a certain disdain understand what was happening in this movie.

The point is clear. The truth sets you free. When you stop lying and face and speak the truth, you change, the world changes, you get healthy, no matter what you have done and no matter what issues you are struggling with. Granted, the movie zeroes in on being honest in just one area, sex, and this is not incidental because sexuality is the area that we find it very hard to be really honest about, but its point is universally true. Health takes its root in honesty. To lie, in any area of life, is to be somehow sick in every area of life.

The blind man in chapter 9 of John's Gospel could be a character from *Sex, Lies, and Videotape.* His blindness is more than physical. He is blind to the truth, not interested in the way, the truth, and the life. But they find him — because he refuses to lie. Truth, Christ, life, light, health, these will find us too if we stop rationalizing and lying. No honest heart will stray far or stay long from the truth.

A friend of mine who in the passion of his youth did a

colossally stupid thing, a thing which is now the source of considerable embarrassment for him, when confronted with his past mistake is fond of saying: "It seemed like a good idea at the time!" I often wonder how different human history might have been had Adam and Eve, after eating the apple and being found by God, hiding, naked, cowering, and ashamed, instead of rationalizing and blaming, simply said to God: "It seemed like a good idea at the time!"

Martin Luther once said, "Sin bravely!" There is wisdom of every sort in that. We are as sick as our sickest secret. The truth can set us free, but we must, at some point, stare our sickness in its face and honestly acknowledge it. Then the truth will find us, just as Christ found the man born blind.

INFERIORITY BUILDS THE SOUL

James Hillman, who is perhaps America's most fertile thinker, suggests that it is our inferiorities that build up our souls. His view is that it is not our strengths that give us depth and character but our weaknesses. Passing strange, yet strangely true, but more of us are rendered superficial by our successes than by our failures, more of us are torn apart by our strengths than by our weaknesses. Why is it like that?

Reflecting on this, I recall a time some years back when I was a young student studying psychology and one evening having the privileged experience of being at a seminar with the renowned Polish psychologist Casmir Dabrowski. He had just given us a lecture on a concept which he called "positive disintegration." His theory was that we grow by, first, falling apart. At one point I raised this objection: "Can't we also grow by being built up by our successes, by taking in positive affirmation and letting it purify us of our selfishness?"

His answer supports Hillman: "Theoretically, yes, we can

grow through our successes, just as easily as we can through our failures. But I can say this, through more than forty years of psychiatric practice I have rarely seen it. Almost always deep growth takes place through the opposite — our deaths, our losses, our dark nights of the soul." He, like Hillman, believed that it is in the end our inferiorities that build up our souls. Hence, an important exercise in the spiritual life is that of learning to listen to our inferiorities.

Thus, for example, it is generally the least gifted member of the family, the one the family is most publicly ashamed of, more than the most gifted member of the family who most enriches a family. Ask any family that has a handicapped member. Moreover, ask any family who has a handicapped member what they think has given them depth, compassion, and understanding. They will tell you, as does Christopher de Vinck in his masterpiece, *The Power of the Powerless: A Brother's Legacy of Love*, that soul comes from inferiority. It is weakness, limit, shame, and powerlessness that bring depth.

What has made us deep persons? What has taught us compassion? Our successes? The things we have been praised for? Those qualities of body or mind which make us superior to others? That perfect body that everyone envies us for? That athletic achievement that is one-in-a-million? That summa cum laude that is the envy of our classmates? That perfect home that is the envy of our neighbors? Have these given us soul? Are these what make us interesting?

To the contrary, our souls, precisely insofar as they have depth, strength, compassion, and hold interest for others, have been shaped by something quite different: the fear that I will gain weight and end up looking like my mother, the shame that I feel because my teeth aren't straight, the birth-mark that I cannot hide, the blemishes that set me apart, the fat around my waist and hips that humbles me, the fear that I am not smart enough, not interesting enough, that my background is not good enough, my phobias, my timidities, my plain and simple inadequacies. These, coupled with the diapers I have had to change; the humiliations I endure in my work, in my marriage, and in my family that I am powerless to do anything about; the insults and taunts I received on the playground as a child; my drunken stepfather: these are what give me depth of soul.

It is not that these are good in and of themselves; it is just that when we listen to them we grow deep. They build up our souls. These inferiorities, these humiliations, are not things to be cured from, things to be solved, things to be ignored, things to be buried as private and past shames. They are to be listened to. They are entries into the depth of our souls.

Daniel Berrigan was once asked to give a talk on God. How do we listen to God? He surprised his audience. He gave no theological treatise; he simply described how he goes regularly and sits at the bedside of a young boy who is deaf, mute, paralyzed, and unable to react in any way to anything that is around him. He just lies in bed, helpless, powerless, unable to say or do anything. Berrigan goes and sits by his bedside. Nothing is said and nothing, seemingly, is exchanged. But, says Berrigan, "I sit by his helplessness and I know that in this powerlessness God is speaking — and speaking in the only way that God can speak in this world." Inferiority, powerlessness, humiliation — forgers of depth, of soul, the voice of God!

RESPECTED WOMAN'S DARK SIDE HIDDEN FROM PUBLIC VIEW

Some years ago, while directing a retreat, a woman, who was admired and respected within her family and circle of friends, shared this story with me.

From all appearances she was the devoted mother, the faithful wife, the dedicated Christian, the concerned citizen, the person who had her life together. That, however, was not the full picture. Beneath that surface of calm, stability, and fidelity, she dealt with an emotional and sexual complexity that had led her many times in her youth and several times in her more recent past to behavior that would, she felt, surprise and scandalize, if they ever found out, her circle of family and friends who saw her as so single-minded, devoted, and faithful.

She was a complex person, partly grace incarnate, partly dark history with skeletons in her closet. She shared with me some thoughts about her "hidden life," thoughts which merit a wide audience:

Often I feel like a hypocrite, I'm so admired and yet there is this other side of me. I worry about what people would think if they really knew everything about me.

I've always been honest in confession, I take consolation in that at least, but what really scares me is the passage where Jesus says, "Nothing that is hidden now will not be revealed." When I hear that, I always imagine myself standing naked, exposed, before everyone, an object of surprise and disappointment.

But something came to me recently, reflecting on all of this, that has helped me a great deal, not so much to rationalize my own betrayals, but to live with a lot less self-pity and anger in my life. What I came to was this. I realized that in my life there are not only bad things that are hidden, but many good things too. If all of my darkest moments and thoughts would ever be fully exposed, those who knew me would be, I think, genuinely shocked. Conversely, though, if all the hidden acts of virtue, dedication, duty, kindness, and charity that I have ever done (which are also hidden and taken for granted, not rewarded, nor properly recognized) were exposed and brought to full light, I think my family and circle of friends would also be genuinely shocked and surprised.

This has helped me in many ways. First, because I believe Christ's words that "everything now hidden will one day be revealed," I try to do a lot of good things quietly, in a hidden way, without needing to be recognized or thanked for them.

Since I have a certain hidden dark life, I want too to have a certain hidden grace life. When the great book is opened and all is revealed about me — well, there will be some surprisingly pleasant shocks as well!

More importantly though, this has helped me eliminate much self-pity from my life. I have always been tempted toward self-pity and resentment because those closest to me rarely notice what I do for them. Most often, what I do (in general terms and for them in particular) goes unnoticed, unappreciated, and is taken for granted.

Worse yet, sometimes other people take the credit for something I did. This used to make me want to scream. Now I realize that if so much of my sin is to remain hidden, isn't it right and fair that so much of my virtue should also remain hidden and unexposed?

There's something not right in wanting all our virtues and good deeds trumpeted publicly and all our sin to remain hidden. Realizing that "everything that is now hidden will one day be brought to full light" has helped me live with a lot less self-pity and resentment.

I can also forgive others more easily because now I no longer need, first, to have every injustice that was done to me by them fully exposed and admitted. It doesn't matter so much to me anymore whether someone is getting away with something — since I am getting away with a lot! Injustices done to me may also lie hidden.

There is much practical wisdom in this simple theology of the hidden life. We all have our dark side even as we have our hidden virtues.

Daily we get away with murder, even as nobody notices the many ways that cost is painfully exacted from us as we live lives of quiet heroism. God knows, and in God's book, the murder is forgiven and redeemed, even as the hundredfold reward is being prepared for our hidden sacrifices. Knowing this, as this woman rightly observes, should lead to a lot less self-pity.

TAKE UP YOUR COUCH AND WALK!

Daniel Berrigan once wrote that if Jesus returned to earth he would pick up the whips he used on the moneychangers, go into counseling offices and therapy groups, and drive out therapists and clients alike with the words: "Take up your couch and walk! You have skin to cover raw nerves; you don't have to be that sensitive!"

That is vintage "Berrigan-talk," so it comes across harshly, even as it underscores something very important. As human beings, we have tremendous powers of resilience, and we owe it to ourselves and to our world to claim them. Otherwise we will never come to community.

We are called to community, to stay with each other. This, despite romantic dreams about friendship, marriage, and community, is singularly the most difficult task that there is. We cannot ever be close to anyone for long without seriously hurting that person and that person seriously hurting us. Hence community depends upon us having the resilience to forgive, forget, bounce back, and live in some joy and happiness *despite* having been hurt and wounded.

And all of us are wounded, deeply so. There are no whole persons. All of us, from the moment we emerge from the womb, in ways physical and emotional, take spills, get dropped, get burned, get rejected, and are abused. Nobody reaches adulthood without deep scars. This damage, as Judith Viorst so aptly puts it, "is permanent, but not fatal!"

Today, however, it is in vogue to live as if it were fatal. So much, both inside and outside us, encourages us to be hypersensitive, and the result is often psychological and relational paralysis — and the breakdown of community. Rare today is the marriage, friendship, family, religious community, parish community, academic faculty, or social justice group that stays intact for long. Invariably someone (and eventually everyone) gets hurt and things begin to fall apart and they all head off to lick their wounds or to look at them in therapy.

Therapy itself can be good. However, and this is Berrigan's point, it can also become an excuse for not claiming the resilience (and, yes, toughness) with which God endowed us and without which we cannot live with each other. Much good is happening in therapeutic rooms and in growth groups today as we get in touch with our wounds, addictions, and dysfunctions, and the systems that help cause them. But there is also the tendency among too many of us to let the therapy itself and the new sensitivity become yet another addiction. When this happens, then sensitivity to our wounds and dysfunctions tends to make us so oversensitive that we become impossible to live with because everything hurts us so badly. We get to a point where we can no longer take the normal bump and grind that is simply part of all living and relating.

Too common today is the phenomenon of claiming one's right to be angry and offended, of stomping out of rooms in rage because somebody slipped and said something that offended our sensitivities, and of refusing to make the effort to come back to certain communities and relationships because "we just can't handle the hurt." There is a time for claiming one's hurts and licking one's wounds, but there is also a time for claiming one's resilience and to get on with the hard, and nonnegotiable, task of living and working together — despite and beyond the fact that we hurt.

In her marvelous autobiography, Therese of Lisieux tells us how her major conversion in life was not religious, nor moral, but psychological. As a child she had always been extraordinarily sensitive, to the point where the most minute slight or hurt would cause her to freeze over and withdraw in tears. She reached a point where this deprived her not only of any bounce and happiness in life, but of physical health as well. She lay dying. There, together with her family, she prayed for a miracle. The miracle that eventually restored her health brought with it the ingredient to retain it, the gift of resilience, bounce, toughness. Looking back from her deathbed, she sees this as the turning point in her life; she was able to live beyond her hypersensitivity. She still remained an extraordinarily sensitive person, but she was, from the moment of that conversion onward, also a person of extraordinary bounce and resilience, finally equipped with what it takes to live in love and community.

We need to pray for that kind of conversion. To be a Christian is not to be some tragic anti-hero, frozen outside community. To be a Christian is to be endowed with extraordinary resilience and a child of the resurrection who is capable of bouncing back from more than one or two black Fridays with a new spirit bathing old scars in a joyous light. Real love and community come after that.

There is something deeply catholic (in the full meaning of that word) in claiming one's resilience. Christ really meant it when he said: "Take up your couch and walk"!

IN PURSUIT OF INNOCENCE

Innocence is not the prerogative of infants and puppies, and far less of mountains and fixed stars, which have no prerogatives at all. It is not lost to us; the world is a better place than that. Like any other of the spirit's good gifts, it is there if you want it, free for the asking, as has been stressed by stronger words than mine. It is possible to pursue innocence as hounds pursue hares: simple-mindedly, driven by a kind of love, crashing over creeks, keening and lost in fields and forests, circling, vaulting over hedges and hills, wide-eyed, giving loud tongue all unawares to the deepest, most incomprehensible longing, a root-flame in the heart, and that warbling chorus resounding back from the mountains. (Annie Dillard, *Pilgrim at Tinker Creek*, 82)

One of the deepest underpinnings of all morality and spirituality is innocence — if not its achievement, at least its desire. Just as any healthy child spontaneously longs for the experience of an adult, any healthy adult longs for the heart of a child. To lose the desire for innocence is to lose touch with one's soul. It is, in fact, the loss of one's soul since to lose entirely the desire for innocence constitutes one of the qualities of being in hell.

What is innocence?

Dillard herself describes it as the soul's "unselfconscious state at any moment of pure devotion to any object." For her, innocence is the sheer gaze of admiration, something tantamount to what James Joyce describes in *A Portrait of the Artist as a Young Man*, when young Steven sees a half-dressed girl on a beach and instead of being moved by desire for her is moved only by an overwhelming wonder and admiration.

The late Allan Bloom, in *The Closing of the American Mind*, suggests that in the end innocence is chastity and that chastity has more than sexual connotations. In his view, there needs to be a certain chastity in all of our experiencing, that is, we need to experience things only if and when we can experience them in such a way that we remain integrated. Simply put, we lose our innocence when we experience things that "unglue" us, that cause disintegration — be that moral, psychological, emotional, spiritual, or erotic. Bloom suggests that, today, most of us, through lack of chastity, have already become somewhat unglued. This, he suggests, manifests itself not just in spiraling rates for suicide, emotional breakdown, and drug and alcohol abuse, but, and especially, in a certain deadness that leaves us "limping erotically," without fire in our eyes and without much in the way of the sublime in our hearts and in our dreams.

A number of philosophers and mythologists today suggest that adult innocence, unlike the natural innocence of a child, has to do with reaching "second naivete" and "post-criticalness." More simply stated, they distinguish between childishness, the spontaneous innocence of a child that has its roots in a certain ignorance and naivete, and childlikeness, the postcritical stance of an informed, experienced adult who can again take on the wonder of a child.

Finally, there is Jesus, who defined innocence as consisting in having the heart of a child and the heart of a virgin: "Unless you have the heart of a child you will not enter the kingdom of heaven." "The kingdom of heaven can be compared to ten virgins waiting for their bridegroom." For Jesus, the heart of a child is one that is fresh, receptive, full of wonder, and full of respect. The heart of a virgin is one that can live in patience, in inconsummation, without the finished symphony. The virgin's heart is innocent because it can live without breaking certain taboos, knowing that, as a child, many of the things that it so deeply desires cannot be had just yet. The virgin's heart does not test its God.

In her novel *The Stone Angel* Margaret Laurence describes a woman, Hagar Shipley, who one day looks at herself in a mirror and is horrified by what she sees. She scarcely recognizes her own face and what she sees frightens her. How can one, imperceptible to one's own self, change and become so different, so old, so lifeless, so devoid of all freshness and innocence?

It can, and it does, happen to us all. Most of us have long ceased being the type of person that the child within us can make easy friends with. It is time to pursue innocence as hounds pursue hares, simplemindedly, crashing over creeks, keening in lost fields, driven by a kind of love.

LITTLE THINGS

Few spiritualities have ever caught our attention and imagination as has "the little way" of Therese of Lisieux. By the same token, few spiritualities have been as badly misunderstood. For a great many people, Therese's little way is something to be praised and revered (who can say anything bad about a child or a pious icon?), but it is scarcely seen as something offering a deep secret to complex, full-blooded, and restless adults.

Recently I received a letter from a reader who shared with me, both in prose and poetry, a spirituality that she has forged for herself. It is a version of "the little way," and with her permission (with a few deliberate redactions to disguise her identity) I share its broad outlines with you:

> I am twenty-eight years old and have spent most of my adult life unemployed, like a lot of other people in this area. I live in an apartment block in one of the most economically depressed areas of England. The complex I live in is large. My own flat is about fifty feet up, right over one of the noisiest sections (which can have its moments, especially at night). People do their best, but the place is still full of graffiti, litter, and dog dirt — not much to look at, unless you like a lot of bare concrete. I can't pretend to be entirely happy in a place like this — there's a lot of noise, a lot of violence, the elevators stink of urine, and nobody seems to have any hope left. Unemployment on these flats normally varies from 60 to 75 percent.
>
> My concern for justice — not only for places like this, but for women, for the unborn, for disabled people, for anyone who needs it — led me into politics. However, the more I go on, the more of a strain I find it. Admittedly, my health hasn't helped, but the real strain has been the conflict between the political mentality and my particular spirituality. In politics, whatever party you belong to, the aim is to get power, ideally so that you can use it to empower others. I've tried to do that, though I've never had much actual power and am growing in the suspicion that even those who do have power are

prevented by the system from ever using it to really help others.

But I've developed a spirituality for this. It's about being vulnerable, hurting alongside people, showing God's strength in my own weakness. In a place like this, I don't see what else I could have. I don't believe at all that there is anything wrong with political power; a close friend of ours had a fairly important political position here and God worked through him in a number of ways. I just find it's very difficult to put it together with being little. How does one fight for peace and yet remain gentle? I ask these questions... and I still stay in politics because I feel if there weren't any little people, some of the big people might start to forget about them. I think some of them do already. So, here's a poem that says what I feel and think....

Little Things

There is a strength in little things:
the snowdrop breaking through the sod,
the echo of the voice of God
in every morning bird that sings.

The balm for spirits crushed and broken
is not made by decree of kings,
but from a thousand little things
like gentle words, like prayers unspoken.

The world is huge; around it rings
the clangor of unending war.
Whatever we are fighting for,
there seems no room for little things.

Yet snowdrops do not cease to grow,
small envoys of successive springs;
the still small voice of little things
brings joy amidst our human woe.

When every day the paper brings
more news of human misery,
Lord, give me strength and grace to be
a voice among your little things.

The kingdom of God, as Christ assures us, does lie in mustard seeds, little things. Thank you, Ruth, for reminding us of that.

WEEPING WITH A WALL-EYE

You may have heard this story before. I have heard it told by James Dobson, Richard Rohr, and a few others, but it merits repetition.

Some years ago, an American research center conducted an experiment with wall-eyed pike. They placed this fish in an aquarium and fed it regularly. Then, after a time, they inserted an invisible glass plate into the aquarium, sealing off part of it. They began to put the wall-eye's food on the other side of that plate. Every time the fish tried to take some food, it would bump against the glass plate and come away empty.

For quite a while the fish kept trying, swimming up, attempting to take food, bumping its mouth, and coming away empty. Eventually, the wall-eyed pike just stopped trying. It would swim toward the food, but just before striking the glass plate, it would turn and swim slowly away.

At this point, the researchers removed the glass plate. But the damage had been done. The fish never ate again. No amount of hunger could drive it to attempt again to eat.

It would swim up to the food and at the last second turn away, not knowing that the glass plate was gone and that it could eat freely. The wall-eye eventually died of malnutrition — surrounded by food.

This is not meant as a sentimental little anecdote designed to make us feel sorry for a poor fish which had the misfortune of falling victim to the cruelties of human experiment, though hearing it does give the heart a wrench. The sorrow it triggers goes much deeper than mere sentiment. This story goes to that part of the heart where we would want to cry and never stop crying, but for the most part cannot. It goes to that part of the heart where we are most damaged and most hardened. That is why it begs for tears even as some of the feelings it evokes bring our wounded pride to the surface and harden us against all softness. Somebody suggested that the reason why men are afraid to cry is that if they ever gave in to what is deep inside them and allowed the tears to flow there would be no end of it. The tears would never stop. I believe that this is true of men — and of women as well. Hearing this story helps us understand why. All of us know what happened to this wall-eyed pike and why it eventually stopped eating — and most of us are in danger of dying from a similar malnutrition.

What an incredible parable this is! What an insight it can give us into why we are starving when love is all around us!

Why this deep well of inchoate sadness within us? Why such affective timidity? Why our chronic distrust? Why are we so limp in our capacity to simply let ourselves be loved? Why are we so debilitated and starving for affection, even as we, and everyone around us, are bursting with desire?

We are dying from a lack of love in a world where nearly everyone wants to love and we are unable to pour out love upon people who are starving for it. There are no glass plates between ourselves and others and yet we cannot really touch. Food is all around, and we are dying from malnutrition. Something is deeply wrong and we are, all of us, deeply sad.

This story, to my mind, says something very important about what is wrong, why we are so deeply sad, and what's to be done about it. And its value is that it speaks to the soul, gently, directly, deeply. It is something not so much to be explained as it is to be felt. Its language and image honor the soul and give it both the space and the respect that it needs to do its proper grieving. Hence, stories like this are badly needed. Today we have too little language and too few images that give our souls the permission they need to feel certain things. Instead we have a virtual library of analytical literature which attempts to explain to us why we are, in its terminology, dysfunctional, chronically depressed, and unfree to simply enter the flow of love and delight in it. It is a valuable literature, good in itself, but it is a clinical one. It examines us the way a doctor would — naked on the diagnostic table, under the merciless glare of fluorescent lights, every mole and scab exposed, and no dignity possible as various instruments do their probing.

Weeping with the wall-eyed pike takes away the glare of the fluorescent lights and gives our tears dignity.

Chapter 9

Structure and Soul, Anger and Grief, Men and Women

The River of Gender

The listless beauty of the hour
When snow fell on the apple trees
And the wood-ash gathered in the fire
And we faced our first miseries.

Then the sweeping sunshine of noon
When the mountains like chariot cars
Were ranked to the blue battle — and you and I
Counted our scars.

And then in a strange, grey hour
We lay mouth to mouth, with your face
Under mine like a star on the lake
And I covered the earth, and all space.

The silent, drifting hours
Of morn after morn
And night drifting up to the night
Yet no pathway worn.

Your life, and mine, my love
Passing on and on, the hate
Fusing closer and closer with love
Until at length they mate.
— D. H. LAWRENCE, "History"

I am an only child, hold my hand, chickenman, chickenman, chickenman, hold my hand. — AMY RAY (Indigo Girls)

162

WOMEN, MEN, AND RELIGION

It is not always easy to read the signs of the times. This is true not just because it is not always evident how God's spirit, and other spirits, are moving in the world, but also because the task itself requires a certain boldness.

When I look at why fewer persons are going to church today or why fewer people are vitally involved in church life, I do not like, nor easily accept, what I see. This brief submission is, however, my attempt not to bury my head in the sand but to name and to face.

The church today is being threatened at a very fundamental level by something that might be termed *gender alienation.* Simply put, this means a lot of people are, consciously or unconsciously, experiencing the church as an affront to their femininity or masculinity.

Mostly this has been articulated by feminism. There is no need to review here the literature that has been produced in the last thirty years by feminist authors suggesting that the structures of the church are in their roots masculine and how this makes it very difficult for many women to remain inside the church. There is an ever-growing swell of women's voices suggesting that the structures of the church, of themselves, alienate women. Their view is that one cannot be fully a woman and participate in church life as it now is.

What is important to distinguish here, however, is that this critique focuses largely on the *structures* of the church. In my experience, few Christian feminists have the same difficulty with the *soul* of the church. Thus, for example, I know women who, while so bitter and angry with the church that they no longer attend eucharist or other religious services, are at the same time deeply religious in that they pray on their own, celebrate religious rituals with others, and are passionately concerned about religious matters. To paraphrase Reginald Bibby, they haven't left their churches, they've just stopped going to them!

What is less evident on the surface, and less articulated, is a corresponding male alienation. Men also suffer *gender alienation* from the church. With men, though, the struggle is less with the structures (which they generally have less of a problem with) than with the *soul* of religion. What is meant by this: alienation from the soul of religion?

In a vast oversimplification, it might be said that in the face of the structures of the church men do not very often feel an affront to their masculinity. Structures are something they understand. Where men often feel affronted is at a deeper level: religion itself appears to them as something un-masculine. Men tend not to cry, and they tend not to go much for church or religion either! One sees this simply by looking at the numbers: women outnumber men at religious celebrations somewhere in the region of five to one. More-over, many of the men or boys who are present (in their own bored way) are there only because they have been pressured to go there by the women in their lives. In many men there is a dark feeling that religion is a feminine thing, something that they cannot involve themselves in deeply without some-how stepping outside full masculinity. They cannot articulate this, but it is present at the level of feeling and its symp-toms are, beyond the boredom and lack of interest already mentioned, the tendency to identify religion with piety and to have, if a male has a confessor at all, only a female one. Unlike his Islamic, Buddhist, or Hindu counterpart, the male in Western Christianity finds it difficult to relate religion to his masculine energies.

In essence, in Western Christianity today we see a double alienation: women tend to be alienated from the *structures of the church,* and men tend to be alienated from the *soul of the church.* This is not true, of course, for all men and women, but is true of enough of them to merit serious reflection. Among the many things it potentially suggests is that in Western Christianity *today the structure is masculine, while the soul is feminine.* This creates problems and also suggests that the solution to the issue of gender alienation is extremely complex.

The problem is not simply that a few radical feminists are angry, or that a few patriarchal clerics are entrenched in power. Rather, both the *structures* and the *soul* of Christianity must be opened to a radical overhaul in the Holy Spirit. Moreover, since the alienation is painful on both sides, this also suggests that we each might take Virginia Woolf's words to heart and adopt a new attitude of sympathy toward the other half of the human race — given that life, for both sexes, is arduous, difficult, and a perpetual struggle.

FRUSTRATED GODDESSES AND GRIEVING WARRIORS

Anger and grief do not make a good mixture. When someone is angry it only makes it more frustrating to have to contend with a grieving person. Conversely, when a person is grieving, the last thing that person needs is to contend with someone who is angry. Yet today, as women and men grow ever more sensitive to issues of gender, that is what to a large part we have to look forward to: anger and grief contending with each other.

During the past thirty years, feminism has been a major influence within the Western world. It is not, however, a monolithic phenomenon. The word "feminist," like the word "catholic," has as many variations as it has individuals committed to its credo. Many kinds of things emanate from feminist circles.

Despite this, there is a common denominator: anger. To be committed to feminist consciousness is to be, at some point, angry. This is not surprising. What feminism helps set free, in the metaphorical language of some feminist circles, is the anger of the frustrated goddess. What does this mean?

We all carry within us the *imago Dei*, the image of God. We are born the divine child, and this, whether we admit it or not, colors every aspect of our lives. It is written into our bodies, our hearts, our minds, our souls, and our feelings. We are gods and goddesses, kings and queens, mothers and fathers, called to create, order, nurture, and bless. This is true of both sexes, women and men. We have the same stamp of divinity within us, the same archetypal brand, and from it comes our mutual vocation — create, order, nurture, bless.

Feminist consciousness tells us that for many centuries now women have been partially (and sometimes largely) frustrated in this. Their call to create, order, nurture, and bless has been too often denied them, denigrated, constricted to a very small arena, and abused or usurped by men. The *imago Dei* within them, the goddess, has been frustrated. Now that goddess is angry.

That anger, like feminism itself, is complex. There is *proportionate anger* (measured anger at specific injustices); *ideological anger* (politically incited and politically correct anger — "the anger of the great march," in Milan Kundera's phraseology); *neurotic anger* ("All of my personal unhappiness is political and the political has destroyed all of my happiness!"); and *archetypal anger* (anger that touches the psychic imprint within which are banked all the frustrations of women throughout the centuries).

When anyone is angry, normally there is some mix of all of these. Feminists are no exception. However, it is the last kind, *archetypal anger,* that is important here. When someone looks at feminism today and asks: "Why are you so angry? Isn't your anger really out of proportion to its proximate causes?" that someone does not understand *archetypal anger,* the anger that is the tip of a pine cone that is releasing the frustration of the centuries.

That, though, is also the case with men's grief. It is interesting that when men's groups meet, the dominant feeling that surfaces is not anger, but grief, sadness. There are many tears at "gatherings of men." This grief, like anger within feminist circles, has many roots: grief for the father that the industrial revolution took away from his son; grief for the loss of the primal circle of intimacy with the mother that coming to male identity necessarily takes away from the male; grief for the gender depression that results from not knowing how to act in such a way that it feels good to be a man; and, especially, *archetypal grief,* grief that touches the psychic imprint within which are banked all the losses of men throughout the centuries. When a man cries he too is the tip of a pine cone — through which seep the tears of every coal miner who has ever died of black lung, of every nineteen-year-old soldier who ever left home to die in a strange country in a heartless war, and of every man who ever had to kill an animal or an enemy.

When someone stands before a man today and says: "Why are you so chronically sad? Why are your suicide rates thirty times those of women?" that person is not understanding *archetypal grief.*

Archetypal anger and *archetypal grief* do not make a good mix. But it is vital that they be understood if we, as men and women, are ever to come to a nurturing and tender mutuality that can help heal the centuries-old wounds of both women and men.

AN HONEST ANGER

Today, for the main part, most of us live in chronic depression. This is not clinical depression, so it is not as if we need professional help or therapy; it is just that there is within our lives precious little in terms of delight.

We live and breathe within a culture and a church that are growing daily in sophistication, adultness, and criticalness. This is not always a bad thing, but it is helping to spawn a polarization, anger, and despondence that is making it almost unfashionable to be happy.

Recently I addressed a national conference of Catholic journalists and tried to make the point that, as a Catholic press, we must address this despondence. After my talk, I was challenged by a woman, a former teaching colleague and a friend, who said to me: "Yes, I am angry, and so are many other women. But you make our anger sound like something hard and calloused, while you make men's grief sound like something soft and sensitive. Is that really fair? Are they really that different? Isn't anger, in the end, just another form of grief?"

I was thankful for her challenge because, for the main part, she is right — anger and grief are not that different. On the surface, they appear antithetical, oil and vinegar, but examined more closely, most of the time they are expressions of the same thing, love that has been wounded and yearns for reconciliation.

Rollo May once suggested that the opposite of love is not hate or anger. The opposite of love is indifference. You can only really hate or be properly and thoroughly angry with somebody that you love. The deeper the love, the deeper will be the anger and hatred if the love is wounded or betrayed. Anger and hatred, initially at least, are almost always a sure sign of love. They are love's grief. Most anger, in the end, is a form of grief, just as most grief, when boiled down to its essentials, is a form of anger.

But not all anger is good and neither are all forms of grief. There are different kinds of anger, and these have parallel kinds of grief. There is honest anger and there is dishonest anger; there is honest grief and there is dishonest grief.

Let me try to explain this, using anger (grief has identical parallels). Honest anger obeys three rules.

First, *it does not distort.* Good anger does let hurt blind one to what was good in the past so as to allow a revisionist distortion of the truth. Honest anger is real anger, it feels and points out what is wrong, but it does not, on that account, lie about what is and what was good. It lets the good remain good.

Second, *it is not rage.* There is a big difference between honest anger and rage. Despite its rather coarse surface and its painful disturbing of the peace, honest anger, in the end, seeks to build up, to bring to a new wholeness, to reconcile something that is felt as fractured or broken. It is a disruptive means toward a good end. Rage, by contrast, wants only to bring down, to break apart, to utterly destroy. Its wound is so deep that there is no desire for unity and reconciliation. The clearest expression of this is murder/suicide, the case where the wounded lover kills his lost love and then kills himself.

Finally, *honest anger has a time limit.* It is not forever. It howls and wails for "forty days," the length of time needed, and then it moves on to the promised land. Honest anger never sees itself as an end, a substitute for the lost love.

It does not make an ideology of itself ("I am unhappy...

and I have every right to be!"). Like the Israelites in the desert, like a pining lover, its every energy seeks for the road beyond, the way out, reconciliation, an embrace that heals the fracture.

Honest grief follows the same rules — and these are important rules for all of us, women and men, who desire to move beyond the present divisions to a new embrace.

NO TRUMPETS FOR MEN

Recently at a workshop that I was giving, a woman shared this at the luncheon break: "I have this secret dream. In it, I blow a trumpet one Sunday morning, and at the sound of that trumpet, all the women in churches around the world walk out! Wouldn't that be something! Wouldn't that send some signal to Rome!"

That is one woman's dream and, given some of the anger that has centered in recent years around gender issues in the church, I suspect that more than a few women nurse that kind of fantasy. For men, unfortunately, no such fantasy, or trumpet, is necessary. Most of them have already walked out. As tough as things are for women in the church, they are even tougher, I submit, for men.

I have suggested that the church suffers because of a double alienation: many women are alienated from the structure of the church, whereas many men, perhaps the majority of them, are alienated from its soul.

I know a number of women who no longer go to church because it is too painful for them, given an all-male clergy and a set of structures that they consider unhealthily patriarchal. Yet every one of these women prays, has a deep interest in spirituality, gives and makes retreats, and has deep religious and ecclesial concerns. They have left the church (or, at least, they have stopped going to church), but they are deeply concerned and involved with religion, with Christianity. Conversely, I know many men, young and old, who do go to church, for whom the structures of the church present no obstacle, but who are, deep down, alienated from religion. They don't pray, have no interest in spirituality, and have virtually no ecclesial concerns. They attend church and church functions begrudgingly, either out of a sense of duty or because they are dragged there by the women in their lives. And then there are still the millions of men who are not, it would seem, interested in religion and do not attend church either. What is to be said about this?

The rather simplistic answer is that women are more spiritually developed, more attuned to deeper things, and more sensitive than men. To my mind, that is a dangerous misreading of the situation. The problem is not that men are more areligious or irreligious than women; it is rather that, within Christianity in the Western world, men have a spiritual inferiority complex the size of the Grand Canyon and this wound is further exacerbated by the fact that Christianity, for the main part, has taken on a female soul. While its structures may be overbalanced toward the male side, the church's soul is weighted in reverse. Simply put: it is no accident that, seen archetypally, the pope wears a dress rather than the uniform of a knight or a soldier.

There are reasons for this, not the least of which is the fact that we were taught to believe and pray by our mothers (much more so than by our fathers), but those reasons are not my point here. My point is rather that, as we try to build a healthier, more whole church we must, with more courage and honesty than have been the norm of late, look at the way both women and men are being alienated from the church, and we must look at both structures and soul. Not to have the courage to examine how patriarchal our structures are is to run the risk of losing many women. Conversely, not to have the courage to examine how matriarchal is our soul is to run the risk of losing even still more men.

In his autobiography, Nikos Kazantzakis tells how as a young boy he was torn between the soft religiosity and piety of his mother and the hard impious anticlericalism of his father. When he was a bit older, he picked up the Bible, intending to read it from cover to cover and then decide for himself what was right about Christianity, the softness of his mother or the hardness of his dad. He tells how he thoroughly enjoyed the Old Testament. Yahweh was his kind of God — passion, blood, war, knives, horses, betrayal, forgiveness, on every page. Then he read the New Testament. He describes his disappointment: "After all that strength, blood, and passion, along comes Jesus, petting sheep and drinking chamomile tea!"

His is not the best interpretation of the New Testament, but his comment is a good one to ponder as we try to renew ourselves as a church. We must retain and balance many dualities: softness and hardness, piety and toughness, water and fire, soul and structure, female and male. God is all of these.

CELESTIAL MARRIAGE COUNSELING

Robert Moore, a man who understands a considerable amount about the symbols that undergird the way we think, recently commented that the mythic task for our age is that of doing some mythical celestial marital therapy. Put into simpler terms this means that we must imagine how in the world of fairy tales, in that other world of magic and enchantment, the great king and the great queen can be at peace with each other.

That is, to my mind, also the great theological (not to mention psychological) task for our time: we must reconcile the male and female aspects of God. We must see and feel God not only as a great king but also as a great queen. Beyond even that, and this is Moore's real point, we must imagine a picture wherein the masculinity within God empowers the femininity there in such a way that the feminine can fully be itself. Conversely, we must imagine how the femininity within God can empower the masculinity there so that the masculine can be fully expressive. That is no easy task, either in imagining God or in imagining human relationships between men and women.

We have, to my mind, no strong model here, that is, no real imaginative picture of how the masculine and the feminine can truly mutually empower each other — despite the claims of some recent feminist theologies that their conception does this. We are far from even a minimally adequate picture of this at the present time.

Theologically, our difficulties begin with the fact that we cannot imagine God as married. The conception of God in all the great world religions never presents us with a married God. Yahweh does not have a wife, nor does the ultimate divine reality within Hinduism, Buddhism, or Taoism. It is not that God is conceived of in these religions as *only* masculine. In all of them, God is either seen as both male and female, at least in their deepest understanding of God, or God is conceived of as beyond gender. The problem is not that the female is absent, but that for the most part within Christianity, Judaism, and Islam (the religions that believe in Yahweh), the female aspect is not integrated imaginatively into the Godhead. In the end, in the imagination, if not in theology, we have a masculine God, a celibate, who has a feminine side to him.

In Roman Catholicism, classically we compensated for this by putting a lot of the feminine side of God into the Blessed Virgin Mary. She was seen as the mother of God — not God's equal or wife theologically, but more or less his wife imaginatively. This had its good points, though in the end it left God masculine and, as the critique of feminism has made clear, a better balance needs to be brought about.

More recent theology has attempted to bring about this balance by imagining the Holy Spirit as feminine. This, however, as many theologians have pointed out, perhaps creates more problems than it solves. Among other things, it leaves the Creator masculine.

So where are we right now? A long way from where we would need to be. Our theologies of the past, for all their strengths and goodness, are on this point lacking balance. The present theologies of feminism are, for all their strengths, on this point too simplistic. They too are in want of new imagination. In both the old and the new — in the classical theology of God in Western Christianity and in the proposals of radical feminism — there still is no adequate picture of how masculinity and femininity can work together to truly empower each other. This is doubly true vis-à-vis how we understand the relationship of masculinity and femininity within the same God. For the most part, on this point, our imaginations are pumping dry.

But we are making progress. We are understanding what is at stake, namely, how important it is to make peace between the king and the queen. We are also understanding how difficult it is to bring together masculinity and femininity in human relationships and in God so that one is not threatened by the other, so that one does not need the other to be subservient so that it can act, so that one is not merely a satellite in the orbit of the other, so that both recognize that they exist to empower the other, and so that each feels itself as real only through the other.

Moore's right. We need mythical celestial marital therapy!

THE GENDER OF GOD

One of the more contentious debates within contemporary circles concerns the gender of God. For centuries, the common, though unreflective, notion was that God was masculine, God the Father! Today there are strong feelings, both ways, about that.

Feminists and others are demanding that the churches change their way of thinking and speaking about God to reflect the fact that God is not any more masculine than feminine. Others, however, are digging in in an attempt to defend the more traditional notion. Is God male, female, genderless? The debate here is both serious and important. Occasionally, too, it exhibits its own sense of humor, as in the case of Janet Foster, who, arguing as a woman, submits that God can only be conceived of as male:

> God is a woman, the feminists cry,
> But any fool knows that's a terrible lie.
> He toiled for six days, spent the seventh in heaven;
> If God were a woman, she'd toil the full seven.
> God can't be a woman, as some people say,
> Or he wouldn't have needed to rest on that day,
> 'Cause since time first began and we women know best,
> Only children and man — and God — need a rest!

More seriously, though, how is God to be conceived of and spoken about? There is a double issue involved in grappling with this — a theological one and a pastoral one. The pastoral questions are trickier: How, concretely, do we begin to speak about God if we cease conceiving and speaking of "him" as male? Do we use gender-neutral terms — creator, redeemer, sanctifier? What would this do, long-range, to our conception of God as a person? Is today, when father-hunger is perhaps the deepest longing within our whole world, a good time to start moving away from the concept of God as father?

The theological question is clear, and that needs unequivocal affirmation: God is as much female as male, as much mother as father. That is beyond serious dispute. Christian tradition is clear everywhere, and especially in the creation story, that male and female both image the likeness of God equally.

Moreover, in discussing the question of God's gender, more important even than explicit scriptural affirmations is the whole question of our theology of God and language about God.

All proper theology of God begins with and grounds itself upon the affirmation that God is, by definition, ineffable. What this means is that because God is infinite, without boundaries, God is by that fact too inconceivable and unthinkable. We can know God, but we can never think God. Our minds can never capture God in a concept. Even less can we ever accurately speak about God. All of our concepts and all of our words, including those in Scripture itself, are inadequate, telling us always more about what we do not know than what we do know about God. No concepts and language about God are even remotely adequate, let alone accurate. We use the revealed language that Scriptures give us, not because we pretend that it captures God with any accuracy and adequacy, but because it is less inadequate than other language and we have been given permission by God to use it — and thus, in the apt words of Annie Dillard, can use it without being blown apart from heaven! But in the end, as the church itself has dogmatically defined (at the Fourth Lateran Council of 1215), everything we think about and speak about God is more inadequate than adequate, more inaccurate than accurate.

All of this is doubly true vis-à-vis God's gender. God is not simply male, just as God is not simply female. Nor is God neuter, a genderless force. All thought and language fall short here.

Given the truth of this, none of our personal nouns or ordinary pronouns can be used about God with any accuracy. Perhaps the best route to go here is that used centuries ago by Julian of Norwich who wrote of God:

> As truly as God is our father, so just as truly is he our mother. In our father, God Almighty, we have our being: in our merciful mother we are remade and restored. . . . It is I, the strength and goodness of fatherhood. It is I, the wisdom of motherhood. It is I, the light and grace of holy love. It is I, the Trinity; it is I, the unity.

In that unity we move and have our being.

INCLUSIVE LANGUAGE REVISITED

God is ineffable. All mysticism and theology work off that premise. What that means, among other things, is that, while God can be known, God can never be thought of nor spoken of in any adequate way.

That is also true regarding God's gender. All gender terms we apply to God ("father," "mother," "he," "she") are likewise highly inadequate. God is neither a male nor a female. Nor is God genderless, an "it." Masculinity and femininity both reflect God, and thus, although we cannot ever find either concepts or words to capture this, God is somehow both male and female. How? We don't know. All concepts and language are inadequate here. There is no way to imagine or speak of God's gender.

Yet we must think about God and speak about God in terms of gender. Up to now, with only a handful of exceptions, we have handled this by applying masculine concepts to God. God was male, at least in terms of language, even if vaguely we kept somewhere in mind the qualification: "This is just a metaphor." Feminism is right in saying that this must change, that it is unfair, unhealthy, that language strongly helps shape our thought and that as long as we keep referring to God in purely masculine terms we will continue to think of God as exclusively male. That situation, God conceived of as purely male, is neither true nor healthy. Hence we must risk new ways of thinking and speaking about God in terms of gender.

However, while I agree with the feminist critique that our language about God, vis-à-vis gender, must change, I am far less in agreement with what many feminists, and many others, today propose and practice as a remedy, namely, the elimination of all gender reference to God in terms of language. What passes today for inclusive language is, in fact, an even more exclusive language. It no longer includes any reference to gender whatsoever, female or male. God is spoken of in cosmic, impersonal, and genderless terms.

I remember a feminist friend of mine once humorously commenting on the classic Trinitarian formula, "Father, Son, and Holy Spirit." "What you have here," she stated, "are two men and a bird!" She intended no disrespect. It was simply a statement of phenomenology. However, the suggestion that we change the formula to something like, "Creator, Redeemer, and Sanctifier," in my view, helps little. We now have two cosmic forces and a bird! What is missing is person, gender, feeling, and any kind of word that might stir an emotion inside us.

We must begin to use inclusive language, but that language must, precisely, be inclusive of both genders. My own suggestion is that rather than trying to avoid all reference to gender, as we are now doing in those places where there is sensitivity to this issue, we try for a language that is truly inclusive. Simply put, we begin to refer to God, alternatively, in terms both female and male and we apply both pronouns, she and he, to God. Thus, we might sometimes say "Our Father" and sometimes "Our Mother." Likewise, sometimes we could refer to God as "he" and sometimes as "she."

Initially, of course, there would be opposition and ridicule. That is to be understood and accepted as a part of any change of this kind. Eventually, however, comfort would return and we would come to think about and speak of God and be comfortable with either gender. We would then be imagining God less inadequately and our faith and our lives would be the better for it.

The problem, in my view, with present attempts to use inclusive language by eliminating all reference to gender is that, at best, these efforts impersonalize God and leave us with a vague cosmic force which no longer has any emotional connection to us. Words such as "creator," "redeemer," and "sanctifier" have no emotional content. Conversely, words such as "father" and "mother" do. Positively or negatively, we feel something around gender-laden words. Moreover, some attempts at inclusive language slander the archetypal masculine by demonizing what is male. No health can result from this and even fewer men will relate to the churches if this persists — just as fewer women will relate to the churches if we do not move toward inclusive language.

We must risk inclusive language. The long-range health of the churches is what is at stake here. But genderless language, by definition, excludes everyone, female and male.

Chapter 10

A Love beyond
Our Understanding

The Wild, Unconditional Love of God

It was the much in Magdalene that Jesus loved.
For, as Mark says,
  "He was too much for them."
Like a woman who loves too much
like an ointment that costs too much
and is spilled too much,
like a seventy times seven God
who forgives too much,
like a seed that grows too much
and yields thirty
    sixty
    a hundred fold.
— John Shea, *The Indiscriminate Host*

When Christ said: "Forgive them for they know not what they do,"
He was speaking of an ignorance that excuses sin. Most of the time
when we sin — we do know what we are doing, but we don't know
how much God loves us — hence we are still innocent through
ignorance.   — Karl Rahner, *Prayers for a Lifetime*

TAKING GOD SERIOUSLY

Several years ago I attended the funeral of a young man who
had been killed in a traffic accident. From nearly every point
of view he died in less than ideal circumstances. He was still
very young, not yet thirty years old, had come from a tradi-

181

tional Catholic family, but had, for the past several years, not been to church, been sexually promiscuous, and died intoxicated. Hardly the paradigm for a Christian death!

I was the presiding priest at the funeral, and as I looked around the congregation, at his family, his relatives, and his friends, I saw not just a deep sadness about his loss, but also a real fear for his salvation. These were good people present, good Christians, who were worried that this young man might now be in hell because he had, by all surface appearance, died outside grace, in serious sin. A woman, an aunt of his, had commented to me the previous evening at the wake: "I wish I were God, running the gates of heaven. I would let him in, in spite of the way he died. He had such a good heart!"

Her comment became the basis for my sermon within which I assured everyone present that this young man, with his good heart, was, right now, being solidly, lovingly, and joyfully embraced by God — not unlike the prodigal son. If we, with our weak understanding and imperfect compassion were able to see through this young man's struggles to the goodness of his heart, how much more so God? Sometimes we do not give God much credit for intelligence, compassion, and forgiveness!

We teach that God is unconditional love and seldom, in fact never, take that seriously enough. Our generation likes to believe that we have freed ourselves from some older fears. God was sometimes seen as someone with a big stick, ready to punish us for every weakness and infidelity, or as someone with a big book, recording every one of our sins in view of some great future reckoning. We have moved a bit beyond this, though not nearly as much as we give ourselves credit for. By and large, our God is still a vindictive God, a petty God, a stupid, noncompassionate God. In conservative circles, God is hung up on orthodoxy, on dogma and morals.

In liberal circles, God is hung up on social justice. In neither circle is God very joyous, understanding, and compassionate.

We are still a long way from appropriating the God that was incarnate in Jesus. Do we ever really take the unconditional love of God seriously? Do we ever really take the joy of God seriously? Do we ever really believe that God loves us long before any sin we commit and long after every sin we will ever commit? Do we ever really believe that God still, unconditionally, loves Satan, and everyone in hell, and that God is even now willing to open the gates of heaven to them? Do we ever really take seriously how wide is the embrace of God? Do we ever believe Julian of Norwich when she tells us that God sits in the center of heaven, smiling, his face completely relaxed, looking like a marvelous symphony? No. Except for rare moments of grace we still believe in a God who is hyperserious, wired, intense, pained, disappointed in us, disappointed in the world, and far from unconditionally forgiving.

Yet the deep struggle of all religion is to enter into the joy of God.

Some years ago, while I was doing a thirty-day Ignatian retreat, my director, a wise, though not very old, Jesuit, asked me to meditate on the scourging of Jesus by the Roman soldiers. He gave me the text from Scripture where Peter out of fear betrays Jesus, denying that he knows him, and follows at a safe distance, pretending he is not one of his followers. Then, just after Jesus has been scourged and humiliated, he turns and looks Peter square in the face.

"In your meditation, pretend you are Peter," my director instructed me. "Let Jesus look at you, really look you in the face, and then come back and tell me what you saw in that face." I did the meditation a number of times, and every time I contemplated Jesus' face I saw the face of someone very good who loved me — my father, an intimate friend, my mentor — but the face I saw showed, besides love, something else: pained disappointment in me. My director made me do the meditation over and over until, finally, in a moment of grace, I saw what Peter must have seen, and what made him go out into the night and weep bitterly, namely, a softness, acceptance, and nondisappointment beyond anything anyone has ever shown me.

IMAGES OF GOD'S HEART

James Hillman once said that a good image is the most open, most exploratory, most suggestibly subtle, yet most precise thing to allow the soul the widest imagination for its complexes.

With this in mind, I submit some images of God as a meditation — to allow the soul some imagination for its complexes.

Recently I received a letter from a young mother who described the disappointment of her little son when she had to leave home for a few days to attend a convention. Her account of her son's reaction to her leaving expresses a healthy motherly mixture of pride, love, delight, understanding, and humor: "Andrew is three years old and is still very much mummy's boy. He cried when I left, and then when I went to hug and kiss him, he went and sat on the coffee table with his back toward me and wouldn't even look at me. He was so mad!"

Imagine how God must feel at times, proud as a mother looking at us! I doubt that in the light of eternity our sullen pouts, our angers, our turning away, and even our dramatic declarings that "God is dead," look much different than does the typical three-year-old who is throwing a tantrum because mummy is going away. I don't doubt either that God, like the mother just described, cannot help but smile at the humor in it all. How delightfully little and silly we must appear at times.

I suspect too that our very littleness itself must at times move God's heart to unspeakable levels of compassion. Again, let me risk an image:

A few years ago, I was visiting some family friends. Their young daughter was about five years old. At 8:30 or so, her mother put her to bed and, when she returned to the living room where we were visiting, she told me that the child would like me to go into her room and say goodnight, and perhaps tell her a story. I went into the room and found a child who was rather restless (since she had to go to bed by herself and miss out on all the activities that were still going on) and a bit afraid (she told me she was always afraid to be by herself, alone in the dark). After sharing this with me, she smiled and said: "But I have a secret that helps me!" Then, reaching under the curtain onto the window ledge above her bed, she brought down a little stuffed horse. "He's my secret!" she said as she kissed him and tucked him under her pillow "Nobody knows about him except me!" Then, looking infinitely more secure and comfortable, she said goodnight and I left.

I am not a man much given over to sentimentality or saccharine, but the purity of the littleness of that moment — that child, alone and restless in the dark, taking security from a cheap, small stuffed animal, her secret horse — stirred in me a tenderness, a love, a protectiveness, and an understanding that physically wrenched my heart. At such a moment, you see a soul, literally, and you see in its very pettiness and smallness its beauty and its largeness. I am not sure what will happen to this young child once she trades in her naivete and her stuffed horse for other kinds of secrets to help her calm her restlessness and to help herself in the loneliness of the night, but I am certain that God, who will always see her as a young child, when watching her will constantly have the same kind of tender wrenchings of the heart that I experienced that night. Our littleness, no matter what our age and what our secret horse, must constantly trigger indescribable pity and compassion within God.

Julian of Norwich, whose intuitions of God most certainly provide the soul with the widest imagination for its complexes, once described the following scene:

> My mind was lifted up to heaven, and I saw our Lord as a Lord in his own house where he had called his much-loved friends and servants to a banquet. I saw that the Lord did not sit in one place but ranged throughout the house, filling it with joy and gladness. Completely relaxed and courteous, he himself was the happiness and peace of his dear friends, his beautiful face radiating measureless love like a marvelous symphony, and it was that wonderful face shining with the beauty of God that filled that heavenly place with joy and light.

How rarely we truly put ourselves under the mercy! Looking at our angers, our solemn sullenness, our littleness, and the secret horses we keep to still our fears and restlessness, I suspect that God's face must constantly radiate measureless love like a marvelous symphony.

WHAT DOES GOD LOOK LIKE?

Years back, as a young professor of theology, I had a dream: to write a book on the question of faith. My hope was to shed some light on why God is hidden to us. Why don't we

see God physically? Why doesn't God simply show himself
to us in such a way that it would remove all doubt? For
a couple of years, in my spare time, I did some research.
I prepared a bibliography on the question, looked up what
many of the saints and classical theologians had to say on
the issue, and I began to ask colleagues and friends what they
thought. One day, sitting at table in our college cafeteria, I
asked a colleague, an elderly man who had been one of my
own mentors and who was now a professor emeritus, what he
thought on the issue: "Why does God hide himself?" I asked,
"Why doesn't God just appear, physically, beyond doubt, and
then we wouldn't have to have faith; we would know God
with certainty?"

His answer took me by surprise, especially because of its
directness: he spoke very gently, as was his style, but after
his answer I decided I would not write that book after all.
"Your question is an interesting one," he said. "If it is asked
by a young person and asked with sufficient passion, it can
seem like a profound question. But it is not, in the end, profound. What it betrays is a profound lack of understanding of
the incarnation! But do not be discouraged. It is a perennial
question. It is the one that Philip asked Jesus. The answer,
therefore, that I will give you is the same one that Jesus gave
him: 'You can look at all you have seen and heard and still
ask that question? *To see certain things is to have seen the Father!*' To ask a question like this is tantamount to looking at
the most beautiful day in June, seeing all the trees and flowers
in full blossom, and asking a friend, 'Where is summer?' To
see certain things is to see summer. To see certain things is
to see God."

With those thoughts in mind, I would like here to offer a
set of questions that Karl Rahner used to ask people when
they asked him about the veil of faith:

- Have you ever kept silent, despite the urge to defend yourself, when you were unfairly treated?

- Have you ever forgiven another although you gained nothing by it and your forgiveness was accepted as quite natural?

- Have you ever made a sacrifice without receiving any thanks or acknowledgment, without even feeling any inward satisfaction? Have you ever decided to do a thing simply for the sake of conscience, knowing that you must bear sole responsibility for your decision without being able to explain it to anyone?

- Have you ever tried to act purely for love of God when no warmth sustained you, when your act seemed a leap in the dark, simply nonsensical?

- Have you ever been good to someone without expecting a trace of gratitude and without the comfortable feeling of having been "unselfish"?

If you have had such experiences, Rahner asserts, then you have experienced God, perhaps without realizing it.

A priest I know tells the story of how he was preaching one Sunday on the parable of the wedding banquet. He was emphasizing the motif of urgency within the parable: "We must respond now!" he thundered. "Tomorrow it will be too late!" A man got up and walked out of church. The priest suspected that his sermon must have upset the man in some way. However, the next day this man phoned the priest. "The reason I walked out of church yesterday was not that I didn't like your sermon. I left because I understood exactly what you were saying. My brother and I had a fight twelve years ago and we hadn't spoken to each other since that time. When you pointed out how Jesus warns about delaying coming to the banquet, I knew that if I didn't act today, tomorrow I wouldn't have the heart for it. I left church and phoned my brother from the first pay phone I found. We got together last night for a talk and we forgave each other!"

What does God look like? Take the fig tree as your parable: when its leaves grow green then you know that summer is near. Look at someone who has forgiven somebody that person has hated for twelve years and you will know what God looks like.

A little girl drawing a picture was asked by her mother: "What are you drawing?" She replied: "A picture of God!" "But we don't know what God looks like," her mother objected. "Well," replied the child, "when I am finished with this then you will know what God looks like!" If we do the things that Rahner suggests, that too will draw a picture of God.

HOW TO GIVE BIRTH TO GOD

Faith would be that God is self-limited utterly by his creation — a contradiction of the scope of his will; that he bound himself to time and its hazards and hopes as a man would lash himself to a tree for love.

That God's works are as good as we make them. That God is helpless, our baby to bear, self-abandoned on the doorstep of time, wondered at by cattle and oxen.

(Annie Dillard, *Holy the Firm*, 47)

That is deeply insightful. God never dynamites his (or her) way into our world as an overpowering superstar who takes your lives by storm. God still enters the world in the same way as Christ did, as the result of a special gestation process that produces a baby that must then be picked up, nurtured, and coaxed into adulthood. Hence the birth and presence of

God in our world depend, at least within the dynamics of the incarnation, upon a certain human consent and cooperation.

Simply put, for God to have concrete flesh and power in the world and for us to have faith in God, a certain pattern must occur. That pattern, modeled by Mary, is the paradigm for God taking on actual flesh in the world. It is also the blueprint for how faith is born into our lives.

What is that pattern? When we look at how Mary gave birth to Christ, we see that there were four moments to this process:

1. impregnation by the Holy Spirit,

2. gestation of Christ within herself,

3. the pangs of giving birth, and

4. the nurturing of an infant to adulthood.

To meditate on these is to take a bath in the essence of Advent. *Impregnation by the Holy Spirit.* We are told that Mary pondered the word of God until she became pregnant with it. What an extraordinary notion! This not only means that Christ had no human father and that, physically, Mary got pregnant from the Holy Spirit but also that Mary so immersed herself in the Holy Spirit (in charity, joy, peace, patience, goodness, long-suffering, faith, mildness, fidelity, and chastity) that she became pregnant with them, their seed took root in her.

She then gestated them into real flesh. In the silent recesses of her heart and body, and not without that particular kind of nausea that is part and parcel of pregnancy, an umbilical cord developed between herself and that seed of charity, joy, peace, patience, goodness, long-suffering, faith, mildness, fidelity, and chastity. Through that cord she gave to that seed of her own flesh so that it grew into an actual child which, at a point, pushed to be born into the outside world.

The pangs of childbirth. With much groaning of the flesh is a baby born. It is always excruciatingly painful to give in birth to the outside world something one has lovingly gestated inside oneself. This was true of Mary, despite any pious treatises that would make of Jesus' birth something miraculously unnatural vis-à-vis birth pangs to his mother.

Nurturing an infant to adulthood. After a woman has given birth to a child, she has a baby, not an adult. This was also true of Mary. Mary gave birth to a baby, Jesus, but what she ultimately gave to the world was the adult Christ. Like all mothers, after the baby was born, she had to spend years nursing, nurturing, coaxing, and loving her child to adulthood.

Our task in looking at all this is not so much admiration as it is imitation. Mary is not an icon to be reverenced, but the pattern for how the incarnation is to continue, for how God continues to take flesh in this world. And that pattern is perennially the same: we must ponder God's word until we become pregnant with charity, joy, peace, patience, goodness, long-suffering, faith, mildness, fidelity, and chastity. Then complete with the morning sickness this causes us, we must gestate them into real flesh within our own bodies and when the time is right, with much groaning of our natural flesh, give them concrete birth into the world. Finally, we must spend years nursing and coaxing that helpless God ("self-abandoned on the doorstep of time, wondered at by cattle and oxen") into adulthood. That is the way the incarnation works.

That is also how faith works. How do you prove that God exists? You don't! God is not found at the end of some logical syllogism or some experiment of reason. God has to be gestated into our world in the same way as Jesus was gestated by Mary all those years ago at the first Christmas.

THE CONSOLATION OF GOD

Few things are as singularly consoling and as corrective of bad theology as the image that is contained in our Christian belief that Christ *descended into hell.* This is, without doubt, the most consoling doctrine within all of Christianity and within all the great world religions as well. *He descended into hell.* What is meant by such an idea?

There is an old understanding that interprets it this way: after the original sin of Adam and Eve, the gates of heaven were shut and nobody was able to go to heaven until Christ came and "paid the price for our sin." After Christ died, in the time between Good Friday and Easter Sunday, he went to the place where all these saints waited and opened up for them the gate to paradise. Christ's going to that place of the dead (mythically conceptualized as a geographical place but theologically conceived of in a psychological/spiritual sense) was understood as Christ's descent into hell, "to the dead."

There is an even older understanding of this doctrine that, while not denying the essence of what was just described, gives the image another twist: the *descent into hell highlights something* very important in the way Christ died. When one looks at Christ's death and resurrection, one sees that in his death he descended into hell in that he went into the place and space of utter alienation, utter darkness, where one is completely cut off from community, life, and God. There, in that place where he was so utterly alienated and alone, he was able to breathe out the spirit of God, community, and life. Because of this we all have hope, no matter how hopeless it might seem.

Let me try to explain this by using two interrelating images and then connecting them to a third one.

In John 20, the fourth evangelist describes how the resurrected Jesus appeared to the disciples. He tells how the disciples were "huddled together in a locked room, in fear" and how Jesus (twice) came right through the locked doors, stood in the middle of them, and breathed out peace. These images are very significant and powerful: *"huddled in fear"; "he entered through the locked doors"; "he stood in the midst of them and said, 'Peace be with you.'"*

In St. Paul's Cathedral, London, there hangs a famous painting, *The Light of the World,* by Holman Hunt. It shows Christ with a lantern, knocking on a door, waiting for it to be opened up from the inside. An edited version of this, made into a holy card, circulates in pious circles. It shows Christ, with a lantern, knocking on a door on the outside of which there is no knob. Inside the door there is a doorknob and, huddled in fear, depression, and paranoia, stands a man who is obviously faced with the choice — open the door and let Christ in or keep Christ waiting outside! The obvious implication is that only you can open that door. The picture suggests that this particular man might be too depressed to be up to the task.

In a way this holy card contains a legitimate challenge. There are certain doors we must open in order to let Christ into our lives. In another sense, though, this is a very bad holy card. If it is right, then John 20 is wrong. After the resurrection, with the disciples huddled in fear inside of a room, Jesus did not stand and knock, patiently saying: "Only you can open that door!" He came right through the locked doors, stood in the middle of the circle of fear and paranoia, breathed out the Holy Spirit, and said: "Do not be afraid! Peace be with you!"

Several years ago, some family friends of mine had a nineteen-year-old daughter who became severely depressed and attempted suicide. They rallied round her, took her to the best doctors and psychiatrists, and tried every possible way of having their love break through the shell of her sickness and alienation. It did not work. Eventually she killed herself. All the love in the world and all the best medicine and psychiatry in the world could not any more penetrate the private hell that she was in. Her family could not "descend into hell" and open up for her the gates of life and community.

But Christ can. That is what the *descent into hell* means. There is no hell that he cannot penetrate, no locked door he cannot go through. When this young woman woke up on the other side of this life, I am certain that she found Christ standing in the middle of her huddled fear and loneliness and that he, there, breathed out the spirit of community and joy and said: "Do not be afraid. Peace be with you! . . . You don't have to open the door!"

HEALTHY AND UNHEALTHY
FEAR OF HELL

Some years ago I read a book by a pious Christian visionary who had visions of the afterlife in which she saw "souls going down into hell like snowflakes." She linked this vision to Jesus saying that "the gate is small, and the way is narrow that leads to life, and few there are that find it" (Matt. 7:14). In her visions, the vast majority of people were going to hell and only a small minority were being saved. Is such a view sound or sick? Does it speak a deep truth or does it insult the nature of God? Is the fear that it potentially inspires healthy or morbid?

Given the current cultural and religious spirit, a majority of persons would, I suspect, protest that any fear of hellfire whatsoever is unhealthy. That, however, is too simplistic.

Jesus assures us that hell is a real possibility and that a certain fear of it is not necessarily morbid anxiety.

What this visionary expresses, however, is morbid. Her vision of "souls going down into hell like snowflakes" contains some very false and dangerous conjectures, namely, that *we can go through this life blissfully unaware of the fact that we are on the road to damnation* and that *the majority of people are going to hell.*

Can we go through life blissfully ignorant of the fact that we are on the road to damnation? Are the majority of people, in fact, going to hell?

The nature of God and the incarnation belie these suggestions. In regard to being unaware of being on the road to damnation, Jesus does warn us that we can, at a point, rationalize and distort our own consciences to the degree that we see truth as falsehood and prefer the misery of hell to the happiness of heaven. That being done, one can, in fact, be unaware of being on the road to damnation. However, even in this case, hell will not be a surprise waiting for a basically sincere and happy person, but will rather be the full flowering of a lifetime of dishonesty, distortion, and rationalization.

Hell is not full of people spending eternity regretting their mistakes on earth, painfully wishing that they had just one minute back on earth in which to make some act of contrition which would enable them to go to heaven. I suspect that hell isn't very full at all and, if there are any people there, they are not regretting their lives on earth, but are looking with disdain and pity at those poor naive folk who have been duped into heaven. Far from regretting their choices on earth they are grateful for how "enlightened" those choices have made them. The quality of truly being in hell is not regret, but disdain for those whose choices have made them happy. It is not easy to go to hell, at least not forever. It takes a very strong person to permanently set his or her heart against love and happiness. Thank God for weakness!

This implies that the majority of people are not going to hell. To suggest that they are is, I believe, a great insult to the Creator. If God is the passionate, all-patient, all-forgiving lover that Christ reveals, then it is unthinkable that God would sit idly by while the majority of people were being eternally lost. If that were the case, God would redo the incarnation!

One might protest here, saying that, if God truly respects human freedom, there is, beyond what has already been given and revealed in Christ, nothing further God can do. This, however, does not take seriously enough the nature of God and the power of God's love.

Many great saints and mystics were either borderline or full-blown *universalists*. This means that they believed that, in the end, there is universal salvation, nobody will be in hell forever, and the final consummation of history will be when the devil himself converts and enters heaven. Their reason for believing this is not the perennially popular (and very bad) argument: "If God is all-loving and merciful how can he send anyone to hell?" Rather they argue from the power of God's love: "God wishes the salvation of everyone and is, ultimately, powerful enough to bring it about. If we believe in the power of love to heal and to create freely its own response, surely God's perfect love will eventually bring even the most hardened sinner to accept it. If human love, weak and imperfect as it is, can melt hard hearts, won't perfect love eventually penetrate every kind of resistance?"

If that is true, and it is, then nobody is going to spend eternity regretting missed opportunities on earth, and people are not going to hell "like snowflakes." A hell that is fuller than heaven is a mockery of God's nature, love, and power.

BOUND TO CHRIST

Gabriel Marcel once said: "To love someone is to say, you at least will never die." That might sound like romantic wishful thinking, but in Christian faith we believe that this is deep insight, an article of faith, a truth of the incarnation. If we take the incarnation seriously, then to love someone is to say to that person: "You will never die because, in this life and the next, you will never be separated from the community of life, God's family, because in accepting my love you are touching the body of Christ just as really as did anyone who touched the historical Jesus. You will never die and you will never go to hell because you are bound to Christ."

That is an astonishing belief! Few take it seriously. Ten years ago I wrote two rather modest articles. I pointed out that the incarnation, the mystery of God taking on human flesh, is not a thirty-three-year experiment, a one-shot incursion of God into human history that ended with the Ascension of Jesus. The truth is rather that, as the body of Christ on earth, we can continue to do all the things that Jesus did and, as Jesus himself assures us in John's Gospel (14:12), we can even do greater things.

Scripture tells us that we are the body of Christ on earth. It does not say that we are like his body, or that we replace his body, or even that we are his mystical body (which would not be so wrong, if we understood "mystical" in the deep sense of that word). Our Christian faith informs us that we are the body of Christ — flesh, blood, tangible, visible, physical, available to be touched, and all of this definitely and clearly residing in nameable persons on this earth. We are the ongoing incarnation of God, the anointed ones of God, Christ.

This, as I pointed out in those articles, has some rather incredible implications — among them that when Jesus walked around Palestine, people were healed and forgiven, not to mention given eternal life, by touching him, by being touched by him and simply by relating to him. If we are the ongoing incarnation, and we are, then this is also true for us (and not just in the sense of it happening through the institutional churches, important as that is).

The mystery of the incarnation is extensive. It is not just the institutional churches that carry on, carry forth, and carry the mystery of God in human flesh. All love that is in grace is the Word made flesh. To touch it is to be touched by Christ; to touch with it is to touch with Christ because it is the ongoing incarnation. From Augustine through Pius XII, we are told that this is wild doctrine, something beyond our limited imaginations and measured hopes. Nobody dares hope for us as much as God has already given in the incarnation. What are we given there? The power, literally, to block death and hell. If we love someone, that person cannot go to hell because Christ is loving him or her. If we forgive someone, that person is forgiven because Christ is forgiving him or her. If children of ours, or anyone else we love, no longer go to church, our love for them and their love for us bind them solidly to the body of Christ. They continue to touch the hem of Christ's garment as surely as did the woman in the gospels who suffered with a hemorrhage. Their end result, unless they reject their bond to us, will be like hers, namely, healing.

Every time I have ever written about this, I have received a flood of letters, almost all of which suggest that what I am saying is dead wrong or, at the very least, horribly exaggerated. These letters generally have one of two difficulties with this. Many people write saying simply: "How can you say this? Only Christ has the power to forgive sins, to heal, and to bind people to the community of grace." That objection is valid enough — except it is Christ who is doing this. We, as St. Paul so clearly assures us, are the body of Christ. Almost as frequent in people's response to this is the statement: "I would like to believe this, but it would be too good to be true!"

Part of the difficulty in believing in the incarnation is precisely the fact that it is too good to be true: God is not hidden and hard to contact; forgiveness, grace, and salvation are not the prerogative of the lucky and the few; we don't have to save ourselves; we don't have to get our lives perfectly in order to be saved; we don't have to make amends for our sins; human flesh and this world are not obstacles, but part of the vehicle to heaven; we can help each other on the journey; love, indeed even human love, is stronger than death; and to love someone is indeed to say: "You at least will never die!"

Chapter 11

Poets, Imagination, the Mother Tongue, and Religious Language

Paschal Imagination

It's my conviction that slight shifts in imagination have more impact on living than major efforts at change.... Everything associated with the heart — relationship, emotion, passion — can only be grasped and appreciated with the tools of religion and poetry.

— Thomas Moore, *Soulmates*

Metaphors are not to be trifled with. A single metaphor can give birth to love. — Milan Kundera, *The Unbearable Lightness of Being*

PASCHAL IMAGINATION

The night before he first knelt to became "the most reluctant convert in all of Christendom," C. S. Lewis spent long hours walking with J. R. R. Tolkien, the famous novelist (*Lord of the Rings*). Tolkien, a committed Christian, was trying to convince him of the credibility of Christ and the church. Lewis was full of objections. At one point, Tolkien countered Lewis's objections with the simple statement: "Your inability to understand stems from a *failure of imagination on your part!*"

If Tolkien were alive today, I suspect he might want to take us all for a long walk and challenge us in the same way. So much of the frustration and stagnation in Christian

circles today stems from a failure of imagination. To let ourselves be led by God through changing times requires, on
our part, great imagination. Lately, this has been lacking, in
conservative and liberal circles alike.

What is imagination? Imagination is not, first and foremost, the power of fantasy, the power of a George Lucas
to create *Star Wars* or of a Steven Spielberg to create *E.T.*
Imagination is the power to create the images we need to
understand and respond to what we are experiencing. We
lack imagination when we stand before our own experience
petrified, frozen, and unable to accept or cope with what is
there; or when we stand before it stunned, benignly unaware
that forces are about to destroy us. We have healthy imaginations when we can stand before any reality and have a
sense of what God is asking of us. A healthy imagination is
the opposite of resignation, abdication, naive optimism, or
despair. It is the foundation of hope. Through it, we turn fate
to destiny.

Today, as is the case with every generation, we are being
asked to *reimagine* our faith life and our church structures.
Unfortunately, too often we are not up to the task. We
stand before a very complex and radically new situation with
either *petrified* imaginations (the proclivity of the conservative: "We've never done it this way before!") or with fuzzy
uncritical imaginations (the proclivity of the liberal: "Let the
new times roll!"). In both cases, there is very little chance
that fate might be turned to destiny, very little reading of
the signs of the times. In the case of a petrified imagination,
there is too much sticking one's head in the sand, whereas
with the fuzzy uncritical imagination there is an abdication
of any critical response in favor of simply rubber-stamping
recent opinion polls. In both cases, the imagination is dead.
Religion dies with it.

But Christ is not dead. He is still "about his Father's business" in the world, the mystery of his death and resurrection is still being lived out daily, and his spirit is still stirring hearts. However we must have the imaginative radar to read where and how this is taking place:

We must be able to look at our lives, our church, and our world and be able to *name where we've died, claim where we've been born, know what old bodies we need to let ascend,* and *recognize the new spirit that is being given us.* That is the job description for the religious imagination.

Looking at history we see that many of the great religious reformers had great imaginations. People like Francis of Assisi, Dominic, and Ignatius of Loyola were able to look at religious life in their day and imagine a new way of living it. The specific way in which religious life had been lived out (for centuries) had died, but religious life had not died! These reformers were able to name a death, claim a resurrection, let (with proper love and reverence) the old go, and then live with the new spirit that God was now giving. Religious life was *reimaged* and, under the vision that came from their imaginations, exploded in a tremendous burst of growth.

Augustine and Thomas Aquinas (despite the negative press they get today) did the same thing regarding how Christian thought could relate itself to pagan philosophies. Today, Gustavo Gutiérrez's imagination has helped shape a new vision of how the oppressed might live out the gospel. Christ, on the road to Emmaus, reshaped the apostles' imagination. We need to let him do the same thing to us.

For those of us who remember another time, the church as we knew it, parish life as we knew it, religious life as we knew it, what it means to be a Catholic as we knew it, and even family life as we knew it are, in the face of contemporary forces, irrevocably different. We can like it or dislike it, but the fact is indisputable.

We can respond to this with a *petrified imagination* ("only what worked before can work now!") or with a fuzzy *uncritical imagination* ("change is always a sign of progress!"). Or, we can respond with a *paschal imagination,* we can look at the pattern of death and resurrection in Christ and then move on to positively and critically shape our destiny by naming our deaths, claiming our resurrections, letting the old ascend, and living with the spirit that God is actually giving to us.

THE SACRED TASK OF POETRY, SERMON, AND SONG

There is an ancient Polynesian creation myth which holds that in the beginning there were only waters and darkness. The supreme God, lo, then spoke and said: "Let the waters be separated, let the heavens be formed, let the earth be!" And, because of these words, creation came into being.

In the ancient cultures which drew upon this myth, the idea developed that words were very important in the ordering of life's events. Since peace and order were initially separated from chaos by words, words are still always needed to do the same task.

Hence, for them, poets and others who could bring the right words to an occasion had a very sacred and important function. Like God's words, theirs too were seen to separate darkness from light and make peace and order out of chaos. Thus, for every important circumstance, if a war was lost or won, if a woman was sterile, if a child was sick, if the people were despondent, if famine was ravishing the land, or if someone was born or somebody died, words were needed to either heal, redeem, bring order to, or properly celebrate the occasion.

In such a view, the role of the poet, seer, and songwriter was a sacred one, and lack of inspiration here was considered as much of a calamity as was famine, disease, and disaster in war. Mircea Eliade, the great anthropologist, commenting on this writes: every new situation comes about by the death of some former circumstance and "a death can be botched" just as a battle can be lost or psychic equilibrium and joy in living can be destroyed. In ancient cultures, it is significant that disastrous and negative situations were blamed not just on impotence, sickness, and senility, but also upon the lack of inspiration in poets, and upon their inability to create or fitly recite poems and link what was happening to what had once happened at the origins of history.

There is much to be pondered in this, and not just because that Polynesian myth runs so parallel to the creation story in the Bible. Deaths are botched and psychic equilibrium is lost when there is lack of inspiration among our poets, preachers, and songwriters. It is no accident that the ancients link lack of poetic inspiration with sterility, famine, and the loss of a battle. When a people lacks proper poetic expression it cannot move beyond its impotence, feed itself, or recover from its losses or its sins. Conversely, a timely (or timeless) poem, a proper sermon, or a well-written song is like a longed-for pregnancy, rain after a drought, and redemption after a loss or a fall from grace.

It is easier to give examples of this than to explain it theoretically. We have all had the experience of hearing just the right words when we felt sterile, senile, filled with obsessive hungers, or fallen from grace. A poem by a G. M. Hopkins, some homiletic prose from a Thomas Merton or a Henri Nouwen, some mystical writing from a Therese of

Lisieux, an ode to joy or a canticle of the seasons from a
Beethoven or a Vivaldi, or a good piece of pop music from a
Paul Simon, serves precisely to separate light from darkness,
to "unbotch a death," and to restore psychic equilibrium and
fertility.

When we see stain on our baptismal robes and hear Ger-
ard Manley Hopkins say: "Generations have trod, have trod,
have trod; And all is seared with trade, bleared, smeared with
toil: and wears man's smudge and shares man's smell: the soil
is bare now, nor can foot feel, being shod"; when we sit at a
funeral and hear a sermon that properly links the incarnate
word that was the life of this loved one who has passed on to
the incarnate word of Christ, a sermon that properly speaks of
origins, incarnation, design, and providence; when in one of
life's many moods we hear Beethoven's *Ode to Joy* or Vivaldi's
The Four Seasons; or when equally confused and exhilarated
by the ambivalences of our age, we hear Paul Simon's *The
Boy in the Bubble,* or feeling tired beyond words and fallen
from grace we hear his "we can't be forever blessed. Still tomorrow's going to be another working day, and I'm trying to
get some rest … that's all I'm trying, is to get some rest!" we
begin to steady somewhat, to revirginize, to feel light separating from the darkness, and we are, finally again, able to get
some rest and face another working day. And, in those moments, we know the sacred creative power of poetry, sermon,
and song.

THE SACRAMENTALITY
OF EVERYDAY LIFE

Christianity teaches us that our world is holy, that everything is matter for sacrament. In its view, the universe is a
manifestation of God's glory and humanity is made in God's

image. Our bodies are temples of the Holy Spirit, the food we eat is sacramental, and in our work and in sexual embrace we are co-creators with God. This is high theology, a symbolic hedge which dwarfs that found in virtually every other religion and philosophy. Nowhere else, save in outright pantheism, does anyone else affirm anything so radical that it borders on blasphemy. But this is Christian thought — at its best.

The problem, however, is that most times our daily lives are so drab, distracted, and fixed upon realities that seem so base that it makes this idea ("everything is sacrament") seem adolescent fantasy. When we watch the news at night our world does not look like the glory of God. What we do with our bodies at times makes us wonder whether these really are temples of the Holy Spirit. The heartless and thankless way that we consume food and drink leaves little impression of sacramentality, and the symbols and language with which we surround our work and sex speak precious little of co-creation with God.

Why is this so? If the earth is ablaze with the fire of God, why do we, in the words of Elizabeth Barrett Browning, sit around and pick blackberries? We have lost the sense that the world is holy and that our eating, working, and making love are sacramental; and we have lost it because we no longer have the right kind of prayer and ritual in our lives. We no longer connect ourselves, our world, and our eating and our making love to their sacred origins. It is in not making this connection that our prayer and ritual falls short.

Among the Osage Indians, there is a custom that when a child is born, before it is allowed to drink from its mother's breast, a holy person is summoned, someone "who has talked to the gods" is brought into the room. This person recites to the newborn infant the story of the creation of the world and of terrestrial animals. Not until this has been done is the baby given the mother's breast. Later, when the child is old enough to drink water, the same holy person is summoned again. This time he or she tells the story of creation, ending with the story of the sacred origins of water. Only then, after hearing this story, is the child given water. Then, when the child is old enough to take solid foods, "the person who talked to the gods" is brought in again and he or she, this time, tells the story of the origins of grains and other foods. The object of all of this is to introduce the newborn child into the sacramental reality of the world. This child will grow up to know that eating is not just a physiological act, but a religious one as well.

An older generation, that of my parents, had their own pious way of doing this ritual. They blessed their fields and workbenches and bedrooms, they said grace before and after every meal, and some of them went to finalize their engage-ment for marriage in a church. That was their way of telling the story of the sacred origins of water before drinking it.

By and large, we have rejected the mythological way of the Osage Indians and the pious way of my parents' generation. We live, eat, work, and make love under a lower symbolic hedge. Most of our eating is not sacramental because we don't con-nect the food we eat to its sacred origins — and, for the most part, we don't really pray before and after meals. Most of the time we consider our work as a job rather than as co-creation with God because we don't connect it to any sacred origins — and we don't bless our workbenches, offices, classrooms, and boardrooms. And our sex is rarely the eucharist that it should be because the very thought of blessing a bedroom or having sacramental sex causes laughter in most circles.

I am not sure what the solution is. Our age cares little for the mythology of ancient cultures or for the piety of more recent generations. The ways of the past, for better and for worse, are not our ways. But we must find a way to connect our eating and our drinking, our working and our making love, to their sacred origins. Socrates once said that the un-examined life is not worth living. It is also not sacramental. Eating, working, and making love, without reflective prayer and proper ritual, are in the end drab and nonsacramental. The joylessness of so much that should bring us joy can tell us as much.

THE MOTHER TONGUE

Hans Urs Von Baltasar once wrote: "After a mother has smiled for a long time at her child, the child will begin to smile back; she has awakened love in its heart, and in awakening love in its heart, she awakes also recognition."

Awakening love and recognition in a child's heart is, however, tied to more than just the mother's smile. just as important as her smile is her voice. Mothers don't just cuddle babies and smile at them; they speak to them, and it is this that is most critical in bringing a child to human awareness. We come out of the darkness and chaos of unconscious in-fancy only when we are *called out* by voices which cajole, caress, reassure, and forever keep luring us beyond ourselves. Very often, during the early critical months of a child's life, it is the mother's voice that does a lot of this. Thus, it is no accident that the first language we learn is called "our mother tongue" for it was its sounds that caressed us and ultimately lured us out of unthinking darkness and uncontrollable chaos. Rainer Marie Rilke says that an infant's journey into human awareness depends upon the mother's voice displacing "the surging abyss."

Language philosophers agree. In their view, language structures consciousness and creates the very possibility of thought and feeling. Before we can speak or otherwise use a language, we are trapped in a darkness and chaos that leaves us unable to think and feel as human beings. We see this clearly, for instance, in a case like that of Helen Keller. In a real sense, it is true to say that Annie Sullivan, Helen's teacher, broke open the world for Helen. By teaching her language, Annie Sullivan precisely took Helen Keller out of darkness and chaos and opened up for her the possibility of freedom, thought, deep feeling, self-expression, and love.

Perhaps no image is more valuable than this one to help us understand the real purpose of the word of God in our lives. All preaching, teaching, theology, and pastoral practice is really in function of this — of letting God's voice become the smiling, beckoning, caressing, cajoling, luring mother, calling the child out of fear, darkness, chaos, and inarticulateness to freedom, thought, deep feeling, self-expression, and love.

The purpose of God's word is not, first of all, to challenge us to charity, or to do social justice, or to live a certain morality, or even to worship something higher and to form community in a certain way among ourselves, valid though each of these is in itself. Christ came, as God's incarnate word, to bring us life, light, and love. Christ came as *the word* to do for us what our mother tongue does, namely, to shape us in such a way that we can move beyond the fear, darkness, and chaos that prevent us from entering the world of love, thought, and self-expression. Christ, as the word, is Annie Sullivan trying to help Helen Keller break through the chaos of being trapped inside herself, unaware of and unable to enter into true human life. It is no accident that the gospels are fond of speaking of Christ as "the Word." Christianity is more a particular kind of language ("our mother tongue") than it is a religion.

My own hunch is that this is too little the case today. In our theology schools, in our church circles, in our religious magazines and periodicals, and in our preaching and religious teaching in general, there is, I feel, too little of Annie Sullivan and too much a using of God's word for every other kind of purpose. If I take a representative sampling of religious language of any persuasion, the preaching, teaching, and writing of conservative Catholicism, liberal Catholicism, social justice spiritualities, academic theology of most kinds, pious devotional literature, new age spiritualities, or the growing literature around alleged Marian apparitions, I find, with a few salient exceptions, precious little that sounds like my "mother tongue." For the most part, I search in vain in it for an Annie Sullivan who, with incredible patience, understanding, and gentleness, is trying to lead me out of the darkness, inarticulateness, deafness, and chaos into which I was born.

That is not to say that what passes itself off today as preaching, theology, and pastoral practice is not full of valuable truth, interesting insights, and prophetic challenge. What tends to be absent is the caressing, smiling, gentle, beckoning mother who is, with the patience and love of an Annie Sullivan, trying to teach me how to speak, how to enter a world whose complexity and hugeness, at this stage, hopelessly dwarfs me, and how to shape my consciousness so that freedom, love, and self-expression are possible. Like millions of other Christians today, I long for the word of God — in *my mother tongue.*

WAITING FOR A NEW ST. FRANCIS

How do we reach the unchurched? What should we be doing in the light of the fact that church attendance, commitment to the church, and simple interest in the church are slipping daily? What do we do, given that both our culture and our own children, for the main part, are not interested in the church?

Today there is a lot of talk, and considerable passion, on this matter. For the most part, however, this has been more helpful in pointing out the importance of the issue than it has been in suggesting effective ways that the unchurched might be reached. There have been some good efforts made, like some of those around the concept of "the remembering church," but, in the end, they have not been effectual. We continue to lose ground, both in terms of impact on the mainstream culture and in bringing our own children back into the mainstream of the church.

I say this with due sympathy, as someone who does not pretend to have the answers on this, but, and the hard truth needs to be accepted here, despite considerable sincerity and effort, we have so far not come up with a language, or an approach, or a program, or even a vision that offers much hope for even a minimal effect on the unchurched. Most of what we have developed which is good — in terms of vision, approach, language, and program — has to do with maintenance, with sustaining the church life that we already have. However, for all our efforts, we have done virtually nothing that has had a significant impact on the mainstream unchurched culture.

So what is to be done? How do we take Christ to the world? How do we take him to our own children? I don't know and it would seem that nobody else knows either! If we did, we could simply go out and do it. For all of our sincerity, efforts, pastoral think-tanks, and workshops on refounding, our imaginations are still pumping dry. Moreover this is not our fault, since as one of the theorists on refoundation, Gerald Arbuckle, is fond of saying: "The new belongs elsewhere!," and we aren't elsewhere — we are here, inside the church. We are incapable for now of imagining new ways of reaching the unchurched, let alone imagining new ways of living together as a church.

So where will our answer come from? My own hunch, based upon how new imagination ("revelation") has often come into the church in the past, is that it will not come from either our hierarchy, our theologians, our pastoral projects, nor as a result of our endless meetings and workshops on the issue. It will come when some wild man or mad woman, like Francis of Assisi, will one day strip off his or her clothes and walk naked out of some shopping mall and out of some city and begin, with his or her bare hands, to rebuild some old church somewhere (or something to this effect). That madness will not only capture the imagination of the world, the unchurched, but it will, again, reshape the imagination of the rest of us, the churched — and it will reshape it in ways that are right now beyond the imaginations of both conservatives and liberals in the church.

My own hunch too, based upon the axiom that "the new belongs elsewhere," is that this wild man or mad woman will not be someone who is of our generation, that is, the generation of Catholics that is so pathologically and inextricably wrapped up in its own reactions to Vatican II, be they liberal or conservative, and all the infighting that flows out of that. A wild imagination is like a wild flower; it grows elsewhere, in unspoiled meadows, far from well-used roadways and city streets. The imagination that eventually truly reshapes our ecclesiology will, I suspect, constellate in people who are already postcritical, who are not shadow-boxing with their own Christian past and with their own fellow Christians. I suspect this imagination will come out of a new convert or out of somebody who, while born and raised a Catholic, has already understood both the awesome power and ultimate emptiness of pagan beauty and needs now to fight neither the world nor the church. This imagination will be truly free to pull from its sack the new as well as the old. I suspect that it will be somebody, like Francis of Assisi, who comes out of the Yuppie generation. But then, who knows? That's just my imagination — and I am not a wild flower! I am one of those Catholics in whose imagination I have, on this point, little confidence.

In the end, the answer will come from the spirit of God, the wildest of all flowers, which grows in both spoiled and unspoiled meadows and can resurrect dead bodies and faith in both the unchurched and the churched.

OUR LONGING FOR RITUAL

A few years ago, I was working with a young man who had just become a Roman Catholic. Little in his background, religious or otherwise, had helped prepare him for this conversion to Catholicism, or at least so it seemed on the surface.

The opposite seemed true. He came from a well-to-do family that was not only agnostic, but also anti-religious. They considered religion, particularly Roman Catholicism, backward, bigoted, and superstitious. Moreover, he had spent a number of years being rather hedonistic and sexually promiscuous, even as he had succeeded admirably at the university and had entered the work world as a very promising young professional. Somehow, God derailed all that.

When I asked him what happened to change everything, he would say:

> I was depressed for a while and I didn't know what to do or how to pray, so I began to occasionally sit in

unlocked churches. Something particularly fascinated me about old Roman Catholic churches. For me, they had a certain mystery and a magic to them. After a while, I started going to mass. That's what led to my conversion. I became a Roman Catholic because of the sacraments, pure and simple. They're magic, they bring power from beyond — and that's what I need. I have seen everything in this world that's not magic and it's not enough. Anything I can understand rationally cannot give me what I need. I need help from beyond the rational!

Sometimes, too, during our talks he would stop my explanation of something and say to me: "Father, tell me something old! I have seen everything in this world that is not magic and it is not enough!" That is an interesting statement because it is a postmodern one. It no longer naively trusts that all that is crucial for meaning and wholeness will be found in the rational, the modern, and the new. But this is a minority feeling.

Most of us are still modern people, adult children of the enlightenment, ritually tone-deaf, and we distrust anything that cannot be rationally explained. Unlike this postmodern young man, we value new explanations more than we do old rituals. We don't trust magic of any kind, especially of the religious type. However, slowly things are beginning to change. Curiously the change is not happening, as yet, in the churches which for past centuries since the Enlightenment have been almost the sole carrier of ritual within Western culture. The change is happening in radical secular circles which are rediscovering ritual. Thus, for example, in some feminist circles, the persons there will look at a woman who has been the victim of a rape or of some other sexual abuse and see that counseling can only go so far in helping her. She needs something which simple psychological therapy cannot provide. She needs a ritual. Hence, they devise some ritual of cleansing. In many cases, the woman gets better. How does this work? We don't know. If we did we could give it a rational explanation, extrapolate the principle, and apply it psychodynamically. But that is the point: ritual works in a way that goes beyond reason. It is like a kiss, the most primal of all rituals. Kisses do things that words do not, and there is no metaphysics that needs to be written about them.

Men's groups do similar things. Sometimes they will look at a man who has not been loved by his own father and whose life is now, consciously and unconsciously, scarred by that fact. Like women's groups they also see that psychological counseling cannot go the distance in terms of a cure here. Such a man needs more than counseling. He needs to be blessed. He needs ritual. Again, often when this ritual is performed, the man gets better. How does it work? We don't know. There is a power in ritual that is, precisely, beyond the rational. Only older, premodern words — words that talk of angels and demons, of sacred rivers beyond time, and of powers beyond our own — can give us some idea of what is happening here. And, indeed, something is happening. Good ritual carries a power beyond what we can rationally explain. There is a certain magic there.

As Christians we have always had those rituals and that magic. We have just had them under another name; we called them sacraments. One of the deepest hungers in our world today is for sacrament, for ritual, for a power that can give us a magic that words, analysis, psychological understanding, and therapy can never give us on their own. The world has seen everything that is not magic, and it is not enough! It is now challenging us to see the shortcoming in the Enlightenment. It is coming to us and asking: "Tell me something old!"

A CRISIS OF IMAGINATION

When Tolkien suggested to C. S. Lewis that his resistance to Christianity was not so much a question of belief as it was of imagination ("Your inability to understand stems from a failure of imagination on your part"), he was saying something important. He was saying that the seat of our faith does not lie within our imaginations and that we cannot sustain our faith by our imaginations. To forget this can leave us open to a dangerous confusion.

Recently at a retreat a woman approached me for spiritual counsel. Hers was a curious quandary: she felt both full of faith and full of doubt all at the same time. She began by telling me that in her mind she was an orthodox Roman Catholic, even somewhat pious even. Yet, try as she might, she could not believe that Christ physically rose from the dead, nor that we will one day rise from the dead.

"I believe that Christ lived on after his death in some way, but his body rotted in the grave. I don't believe the tomb was empty. Likewise with us. I believe in immortality, but not in resurrection. If I can't believe that, and I can't and I know I never will, does that make me an atheist? Am I losing my faith?"

Looked at superficially, it might appear that she was losing her faith, at least in that she was unable to believe in some nonnegotiable part of the creed. Such a judgment, though, can be quite simplistic. My suggestion to her was in line with Tolkien's comment to C. S. Lewis. Her struggles were much more with her imagination and its incapacity to give her a mental construct of resurrection than they were with believing in the resurrection. What is the difference?

Imagine yourself lying in bed some night. You have just had a very good time of prayer. You are flooded with feelings and images about God. You have strong, clear feelings that God exists. On that particular evening you have no faith doubts — you can feel the existence of God.

Now imagine another night, a darker one. You wake up from a fitful sleep and are overwhelmed by the sense that you do not believe in God. You try to convince yourself that you still believe, but you cannot. Every attempt to imagine that God exists and to feel God's presence comes up empty. You feel empty and you feel the emptiness of the world itself. Try as you may, you cannot shake the feeling that you no longer believe. Try as you may, you can no longer regain the solid ground you once stood on. Try as you may, you can no longer make yourself feel the existence of God.

Does this mean that on one of these nights you have a strong faith and on the other you have a weak one? No. On the one night you have a strong imagination, and on the other you have a weak one. On the one night you can imagine the presence of God, and on the other night you cannot imagine it. Imagination is not faith.

Daniel Berrigan, in his usual colorful manner, states the issue laconically, crassly, but accurately: "Where does your faith live? In the head? In the heart?"

"Your faith," he assures us, "is rarely where your head is at, just as it is rarely where your heart is at. Your faith is where your ass is at! Where are you living? What are you doing? These things — our actions, our charity, our morality — are what determine whether we believe or not."

Passing strange, and strangely true, the posterior is a better indication of where we stand with these than are the head and the heart. For we all have the experience of being within certain commitments (a marriage, a family, a church) where at times our heads and our hearts are not — but we are!

The head tells us this doesn't make sense; the heart no longer has the type of feelings that would keep us there; but we remain there, held by something deeper, something beyond what we can explain or feel. This is where faith lives and this is what faith means.

The woman who sought spiritual counsel from me did believe in the resurrection because, by almost all indicators, she lived her life in the light of it. Her problem was that her imagination could not picture it. She, like all of us, suffers the poverty of a finite imagination trying to picture the infinite. This, however, should never be confused with loss of faith.

Chapter 12

Praying in Life and Letting Life Pray through Us

A Vespers for the World

A Time to Pray

I got up quite early one morning
And rushed right into the day.
I had so much to accomplish
I took no time out to pray.

The problems just tumbled about me,
And heavier came every task.
"Why doesn't God help me?" I wondered;
He said: "Why, you didn't ask!"

I saw naught of joy or of beauty;
The day sped on gray and bleak.
I asked: "Why won't the Lord show me?"
He said: "But you didn't seek!"

I tried to come into God's presence;
I used all my keys at the lock.
God gently, lovingly chided,
"My child, why didn't you knock?"

I woke up quite early this morning
And paused ere entering the day.
There was so much to accomplish
I had to take time to pray. Amen.

— Anonymous

Hang on to me, Lord, or I will certainly slip away from you.

— Keith Clark

PROVIDENCE AND
THE CONSPIRACY OF ACCIDENTS

Some years ago in a class I was teaching a woman shared an interesting story.

She had been raised in a religious home and had been a pious and a regular churchgoer. During her years at the university, however, her interest and practice in religion had progressively slipped, so that by the time of her graduation she no longer attended church or prayed. This indifference to prayer and churchgoing continued for several years after her graduation. Her story focused on how all that changed.

One day, four years after giving up all practice of prayer and churchgoing, she flew to Colorado to spend some time with a married sister and to do some skiing. She arrived on a Saturday evening, and the next morning, Sunday, her sister invited her to go to mass with her. She politely refused and went skiing instead.

On her first run down the ski slope she hit a tree and broke her leg. Sporting a huge cast, she was released from the hospital the following Saturday. The next morning her sister again asked her to come to mass with her. This time ("there wasn't much else to do") she accepted the invitation. As luck would have it, it was Good Shepherd Sunday. As chance would have it, there happened to be a priest visiting from Israel. He could not see her, complete with cast, sitting in the pews, and yet he began his sermon this way:

> There is a custom among shepherds in Israel that existed at the time of Jesus and is still practiced today that needs to be understood in order to appreciate this text. Sometimes very early on in the life of a lamb, a shepherd senses that it is going to be a congenital stray, that it

will forever be drifting away from the herd. What that shepherd does then is deliberately break its leg so that he has to carry it until its leg is healed. By that time, the lamb has become so attached to the shepherd that it never strays again.

"I may be dense!" concluded this woman, "but, given my broken leg and all this chance coincidence, hearing this woke something up inside me. Fifteen years have passed since then and I have prayed and gone to church regularly ever since." John of the Cross once wrote, "The language of God is the experience God writes into our lives." James Mackey once said that divine providence is "a conspiracy of accidents." What this woman experienced that Sunday was precisely the language of God, divine providence, God's finger in her life through a conspiracy of accidents.

Today this concept of divine providence is not very popular. Our age tends to see it connected to an unhealthy fatalism ("If God wants my child to live he will not let her die — we won't take the blood transfusion!"), an unhealthy fundamentalism ("God sent AIDS into the world as a punishment for our sexual promiscuity!"), and an unhealthy theology of God ("God sends us natural and personal disasters to bring us back to true values!")

It is good that our age rejects such a false concept of providence, because God does not start fires, or floods, or wars, or AIDS, or anything else of this nature. Nature, chance, human freedom, and human sin bring these things to pass. However to say that God does not initiate or cause these things is not the same thing as saying that God does not speak through them. God speaks through chance events, both disastrous and advantageous ones. Past generations, like my parents' generation, more easily understood this.

For example, my parents were farmers. For them, as for Abraham and Sarah of old, there were no accidents. There was only providence and the finger of God. If they had a good crop, God was blessing them. If they had a poor crop, well, they concluded that God wanted them to live on less for a while, and for a good reason. And they would always, in the deep parts of their minds and hearts, figure out that reason.

That is a deep form of prayer. In the conspiracy of accidents that makes up what looks like ordinary secular life, the finger of God is writing. We are children of Israel and children of Christ (and of our mothers and fathers in the faith) when we look at each and every event in our lives and ask ourselves: "What is God saying to us in all of this?"

THE ILLUSION OF FAMILIARITY

Some years ago, a confrere of mine, Jerome "Harry" Hellman, O.M.I., wrote a simple, unpretentious poem which he dedicated to his ten-year-old niece after she had given him a tour of the rather humble prairie town in which she lived. Entitled: To Sheryl, My Niece, Aged 10, On Guiding Me Through the Town of Virden, it reads like this:

> I wish someone like you
> could have guided Adam through
> his first fact-finding tour
> or his Father's store
> eons before
> and named
> much more than claimed
> things as his own
> or told us what they're for.

We both know Adam's handicap:

he had no niece —

nor patience, nor the peace
to wait for one.

But this he could have done:

Called upon his little girl
to come along
not set out alone
to claim
and *name*
and *number*
when his first call
clearly was
to *ponder*
and
to *wonder.*

These words echo those of Elizabeth Barrett Browning, who, as we have seen, once said that the earth is ablaze with the fire of God, but only those who see it take their shoes off; the rest sit around and pick blackberries! Her words themselves echo God's words to Moses at the burning bush: "Take your shoes off because the ground you are standing on is holy ground."

Ordinary ground is holy. There is more than enough mystery, secret, marvel, and miracle ablaze in ordinary reality. Unfortunately, most of the time we do not see this because we stand before it trying to claim, name, number, psyche out, and render familiar — when our true task is, instead, to ponder and to wonder. This is an irreverence that fatigues the soul.

Irreverence lies at the root of all sin, and taking-for-granted lies at the root of all irreverence. We begin to take things for granted at the precise moment when we no longer approach life with eyes of a ten-year-old who can look at a small town and still see its rich secrets. It is then, when pondering and wondering are lost, that we become bored, cynical, and restless with our lives and begin to feel that reality holds no secrets, that it is less than marvelous and worthwhile, that, as Margaret Atwood once put it, we're stuck here in a country of thumbed streets and stale buildings, where there is nothing spectacular to see and the weather is ordinary — and where love occurs in its pure form only on the cheaper of the souvenirs. At the root of boredom and cynicism lies the death of wonder. Familiarity deadens the soul. It also spawns our resentments.

True contemplatives, mystics, and children never live the illusion of familiarity. That is why they are never bored, cynical, or resentful. For them, there are no hick towns, God-forsaken places, or ordinary marriage partners and ordinary children who can be taken for granted and rendered familiar. For them, there is only holy ground, the extraordinary, miracle in ordinary life. They, in the words of G. K. Chesterton, "have learned to look at things familiar until these look unfamiliar again."

Karl Rahner was once asked whether he believed in miracles. "I don't believe in them," he replied. "I *rely* on them to get me through daily life!" There's a secret wisdom worth contemplating.

OF ORANGES AND PENNIES

This summer on a couple of occasions a particular skepticism of mine was assaulted. I am one of those people whose faith allows God to do big, earth-shaking historically significant, miracles — the Red Sea and the resurrection of Jesus — but expects that, save for these interventions every ten thousand years or so, God leaves everyday life pretty much alone. So it was with considerable skepticism that I sat in chapel one day and heard one of our most respected Oblate missionaries share this story.

Some twenty-five years ago, he had been in charge of two northern missions which were a considerable distance apart. In winter he made the trip between them by dogsled. Since the trip was too long to make in one day, he built for himself a rough shack halfway in between them; on each trip, he would spend one night.

Each spring, after the snow had melted, he would have to go back there and take out all the things inside the shack (stove, bedding, cooking utensils, and so on) so that these would not get stolen during the summer months. One spring day, he returned to the shack to collect these things for the summer. He came on horseback, stayed overnight, and in the morning packed all the things on to a sled-like contraption that he hooked behind the horse. He then set off for the day-long journey home and, because the horse was already pulling a huge load, he was on foot.

The day was unusually hot and, despite drinking water regularly, he slowly began to feel dehydrated. He reached the main road at 9 p.m. exhausted. Luck was on his side and, just after reaching that road, a truck chanced to come by, and its driver volunteered to take all of his supplies to town for him.

With his horse now free of its load, the priest was able again to climb on its back and rest from his marathon walk. However he was still two hours from home, on horseback now, but dehydrated and exhausted. Riding along in this state, he slowly became obsessed with the craving for an orange, a cold orange. Over and over in his mind, there was the image of himself sinking his teeth into a cool, succulent orange. He said a little prayer to God, half wishing to find an orange.

A short time later he looked down the road, this aban-doned dirt road in the middle of nowhere, and saw an orange gleaming in the moonlight. He was so sure that it was an illusion that he continued riding right along. Then, more to check his sanity than in the hope of finding an orange, he turned back and got off the horse.

Incredible! There was an orange, cool, whole, delicious, just as he had fantasized. He peeled it and ate it. A mile later, another orange appeared: and a mile after that, still another one. A mile apart from each other, "God gave" him four oranges that night. At least that is how he interprets it!

I believe this story because I trust the sanity and sanc-tity of the man who told it, even though I am not much for believing in oranges inexplicably appearing at night on abandoned roads!

Less than a month later, I was visiting one of our retired priests who lives by himself in a small city on the West Coast. He is a man of extraordinary simplicity and deep prayer. I spent some hours sitting with him in his apartment, listening to him describe how he goes up into the hills every morning to watch the sunrise because, as he put it, "in the refraction of light, I see God." He invited me to go out for supper with him, and as we were walking toward the restaurant my eyes chanced to see a penny on the sidewalk. I bent to pick it up, saying: "This is one of my superstitions. If I find a penny, I think I will be lucky that day!"

"It's not a superstition," he told me. "God is blessing you. I know it because before we get to the restaurant you will find another penny. When God blesses us we find two pennies." The agnostic part of me was still dealing with his "seeing God in the refraction of light" when he gave me this assurance that God blesses us by giving us not one but two pennies. Really? Yes, it happened! Just as we got to the door of the restaurant, I looked down and there was a second penny! Who am I to doubt it!

Coincidence? Piety gone over the edge? Have I been working too hard lately? Does God drop oranges on roads and pennies on sidewalks? Somebody once said that the only difference between mystics and psychotics is that mystics are more careful about whom they talk to. As clever as that sounds, it is wrong. The difference has nothing to do with whom they talk to, but with the fact that God is real, that the world of the supernatural actually exists, and that God's providence includes everyday miracles, oranges, and pennies.

INTERRUPTIONS, OUR REAL WORK

David Steindl-Rast commented that we tend to be resentful when things interrupt our work until we realize that, oftentimes, *interruptions are our real work.*

Most of us tend to be impatient and resentful, sometimes deeply so, when our plans are interrupted by demands which deflect our energies from what we would like to be doing. Sometimes this is minor: an unexpected phone call interrupts our work or our favorite TV program. Sometimes the interruption is major: an unwanted pregnancy interrupts our career or education; economic demands interrupt our plans to be a writer or an artist; the demands of a family interrupt our chance to travel, to see movies and plays, and to have the hobbies and recreations we would like; or the loss of health interrupts our career.

Countless things, big and small, constantly derail our agendas, force us to alter our plans, and slowly kill our dreams.

Very often we are resentful: "If only! If only this hadn't happened! Now I have to wait to go back to school, to resume my career. Now I'll never have a chance to fulfill my dream."

Sometimes in middle age, or even earlier, this resentment takes a more radical form: "I've wasted my life. I've been a victim of circumstance, I've given in to the demands of others, and now I'll never get the chance to do what I really wanted to do." Sometimes, however, as Steindl-Rast points out, the opposite happens. Instead of resentment there is gratitude. We realize that the interruptions, so unwelcome at the time, were really salvation and, far from derailing us from our real agenda, they were our real agenda.

You may have known individuals or families where an unplanned pregnancy suddenly turns all plans (economic, career, travel, new house) upside down. Initially there is some bitterness and resentment. Later on the unwanted interruption turns into a much wanted and loved child who creates a happiness in life that dwarfs what might have resulted had original plans not been derailed by that interruption.

In his biography of C. S. Lewis, A. N. Wilson describes how Lewis's life as a teacher and writer during virtually all of his productive years was interrupted by the demands of his adopted mother, who made him do all the shopping and housework and demanded hours of his time daily for domestic tasks. Lewis's own brother, Warnie, who also lived in the household (and who generally refused to be interrupted) laments this fact in his diaries and suggests that Lewis could have been much more prolific had he not had to spend literally thousands of hours shopping, walking the dog, and doing domestic chores.

Lewis himself, however, gives us a far different assessment. Far from resenting these interruptions, he is grateful for them and suggests that it was precisely these domestic demands that kept him in touch with life in a way that other Oxford dons (who never had to shop and do housework) were not. Historians like Wilson agree and suggest that it was because of these interruptions, which kept Lewis's feet squarely on the ground, that Lewis came to insights which appeal so universally.

What initially is experienced as an unwanted interruption can, in the end, be our real agenda, though this is not always true. Our lives are not meant to be left to pure circumstance and fate. We must also actively choose and create destiny. It is not always good to accept whatever happens. We have dreams and talents, and these are God-given, and so we must fight too for our agenda.

However, we must look always for the hand of providence in our interruptions. These often constitute a conspiracy of accidents within which God guides our lives. If we were totally in control of our own agendas, if we could simply plan and execute our lives according to our own dreams with no unwanted derailments, I fear that many of us would (slowly and subtly) become very selfish and would (also slowly and subtly) find our lives empty of simple joy, enthusiasm, family life, and real community. We do not live by accomplishment alone!

The very word "baptism" means derailment. Christ baptizes Peter on the rock when he tells him: "Because you said you love me, your life is now no longer your own. Before you said this, you fastened your belt and you walked wherever you liked. Now, others will put a belt around you and take you where you would rather not go." To submit to love is to be baptized — and to let one's life be forever interrupted. To not let one's life be interrupted is to say no to love.

C. S. Lewis once said that we will spend most of eternity thanking God for those prayers of ours that he didn't answer.

Along the same lines, I suspect we will spend a good part of eternity thanking God for those interruptions that derailed our plans but that baptized us into life and love in a way we could never have ourselves planned or accomplished.

Lewis also once stated that God's harshness is ultimately kinder than human gentleness and that God's compulsion is our liberation. In our interruptions, not infrequently, we experience this.

PROPHETIC MOURNING

Mourn, my people, mourn. Let your pain rise up in your heart and burst forth in you with sobs and cries. Mourn for the silence that exists between you and your spouse. Mourn for the way you were robbed of your innocence. Mourn for the absence of a soft embrace, an intimate friendship, a life-giving sexuality. Mourn for the abuse of your body, your mind, your heart. Mourn for the bitterness of your children, the indifference of your friends, your colleagues' hardness of heart. Mourn for those whose hunger for love brought them AIDS, whose desire for freedom brought them to refugee camps, whose hunger for justice brought them to prisons. Cry for the millions who die from lack of food, lack of care, lack of love.... Don't think of this as normal, something to be taken for granted, something to accept.... Think of it as the dark force of Evil that has penetrated every human heart, every family, every community, every nation, and keeps you imprisoned. Cry for freedom, for salvation, for redemption. Cry loudly and deeply, and trust that your tears will make your eyes see that the Kingdom is close at hand, yes, at your fingertips! (Henri Nouwen, *New Oxford Review,* June 1992)

Today we are called to mourn! There are many aspects to this. As Nouwen rightly points out, we must mourn so that we do not accept as normal the hell that so often makes up earth. To properly cry is to see injustice, indifference, lack of love, and hardness of heart for what they are: evil, living in each of us, in need of redemption.

But this prophetic call to mourn is also the call for us to mourn properly the poverty of our own lives, to stop torturing others with blame, ourselves with self-hatred, and God with unfair expectations because, this side of eternity, we live lives not only of quiet desperation but of chronic disappointment. On this side of eternity, there is for us no such thing as a clear-cut pure joy, and we need to accept and healthily mourn that fact.

Mourn, my people, mourn — or else you will give in to blame and fill with self-hatred, restlessness, and bitterness.

Mourn because your life cannot not be inadequate, that here, in this life, all symphonies remain unfinished, that you cannot help but live in a certain vale of tears.

Mourn because you cannot not disappoint your loved ones — and cannot help but be disappointed by them.

Mourn because you can never live with or love anyone for long without seriously hurting him or her.

Mourn that the good you want to do, you end up not doing and the evil you want to avoid, you end up doing. Mourn the stains in your baptismal robes.

Mourn what might have been, all that you missed out on in life while you were doing something else.

Mourn your restless heart, the fact that no spouse or family or friends can ever take your loneliness away.

Mourn that you are so different from others, that you cannot help but irritate them, anger them, and make them impatient with you.

Mourn your lack of gratitude, that you can so easily take what is most precious for granted, that you can so blindly seize as owed what's given as gift, that charity is most difficult with those you most owe it to.

Mourn your lack of prayer, your infinite capacity for distraction, and the heartaches and headaches that make you think about everything but God.

Mourn your lack of hope, all the life that has been crucified in you, all those dead spots that have taken the bounce out of your step, the light out of your eyes, and the expectation out of your heart. Mourn that you no longer believe in the resurrection!

There is a Chinese axiom that says: "After the ecstasy, go do the laundry!" In a culture and a church too full of bitterness, anger, and frustrated dreams, we need to properly mourn our losses so that we can hear an important prophetic message: 99 percent of life is doing the laundry and waiting for the ecstasy — and that is okay.

A PRAYER FOR PEACE

Lord, our God...

We come to you in helplessness.
We have at this time
    no prophet, priest, prince, or leader.
You alone are our God... help us, who are alone
and have no one to help us but you.

We ask you for the gift of prayer ...

May this lifting of our words, hands, and hearts,
    this acknowledgment of helplessness,
       open us up to insight and strength beyond
        ourselves.
May it link us to all sincere hearts
    on both sides of this conflict.
May it become part of a conspiracy of compassion,
    a prayer of many hearts and many places.
May it call us to be on your side
    rather than ask you to be on ours.
May it be a prayer that deeply respects those whose
    hearts are different from our own.
May it be a prayer embracing the feelings of all
    while discerning good from evil in that embrace.

We pray for an end to war ...

Let grace soften our hearts
    and the hearts of our leaders.
Lead them and us to the type of truth that sets us free
    beyond the tyranny of our greed
        and the structures that divide us.
Lead us to the type of love
    that makes both for charity and justice.

We pray for the victims of war ...

Help us to be in solidarity and displacement
    with all whose lives, dreams, and homes
       are being destroyed.
Receive into your embrace those who are dying;
    give them the peace
       denied them in this life.

Touch with healing the wounded
and look with pity on our mother, earth;
restore to her
the freshness of her virginity
and the fullness of her fertility.

We pray for a new order....

May your kingdom come
so that all people of sincere will
become one community of heart.
Breathe into us your spirit...
charity, joy
peace, patience
goodness, long-suffering
fidelity, mildness, chastity
so that war among us becomes unthinkable.
Give us what we in our helplessness
cannot give ourselves and
help us in our helplessness
to remember that
the true weapons against war
are faith, prayer, fasting, and love.

We pray for courage and guidance...

Make this prayer more than privatized wishing
turn our wishes to hope
and let that hope confront the powers of war
so that
our love will be more than sentiment
our confrontation more than anger
our anger more than self-righteousness
and our righteousness that of your gospel.

Give us peace...

Teach us that peace which surpasses our understanding
which is not about winning or losing
and power and effectiveness,
but which comes when we
open our lives and our hearts
to your invitation to...

"Receive and give thanks
break and share."

Amen.

A VESPERS FOR THE WORLD...

Lord, God, as evening draws near, draw me to yourself in prayer. Draw me to you as earth, for I am its child, the world in microcosm. In my sincerity see its goodness; in my dishonesty see its sin. Make what is in my heart a prayer.

First Psalm

Unless you build the house, in vain do we labor.
Unless you guard the city, in vain do we keep vigil.
In vain is our earlier rising, our going later to rest.
You give to your beloved while they sleep.
All fruit is a gift from you.
Without you we can do nothing.

Psalm Prayer

Lord, the world's self-reliance, its blindness to you, is my self-absorption, my greedy ambition, my lack of time for you. I am forever too preoccupied to pray, too lacking in faith to trust in you. Help me to know that unless you build the building, all effort is vain.

Second Psalm

I have stilled and quieted my soul, like a weaned child
      at its mother's breast.
Like a weaned child, still and at peace,
      even so is my soul within me.
My soul is longing for your peace
      near to you my God.

Psalm Prayer

Lord, my restlessness, my compulsion, my need to find things
to still my many longings, is the earth's disquiet. I bring you
this unfreedom, Lord. Let us come to peace at your breast.
Give us simple rest, quieted souls. Accept our tiredness and
dissipation with sympathy for we are at the mercy of the fires
within us. Let your spirit pray through our restlessness.

Third Psalm

Praise the Lord all you nations
      Glorify him all you peoples
Strong is his love for us
      His fidelity endures forever.

Psalm Prayer

Lord, open our eyes to divinity, to acknowledge you as God.
Let us see in your greatness that which lies beyond our own
limit and self-preoccupation. Let the glory of the heavens
dwarf the worries of this earth. Give us, your children, delight.

Reading

Comfort, O comfort my people, says your God. Speak tenderly
to Jerusalem, and tell her that she has served her term, that
her penalty is paid. (Isa. 40:1–2)

Responsory

Through Christ the new power of the resurrection has come into our world.

Canticle of Mary

My soul proclaims the greatness of the Lord.
>He looks with favor on the lowly.
>He exalts the poor and brings down the rich.
>He loves the humble and scatters the proud.
>His promise can be trusted.

Intercessions

For the poor, for those who bore the heat of this day, the oppressed, the depressed, the hungry, the lonely, the sick, and the dying,
>*Renew us through the power of your resurrection.*
For the leaders in society and in the church that they may be guided by the common interest and not by self-interest,
>*Renew us through the power of your resurrection.*
For a community that is polarized: lead us toward a wider understanding, forgiveness, and community,
>*Renew us through the power of your resurrection.*
For our loved ones, for those who rely on us for prayer and support and for those upon whom we rely,
>*Renew us through the power of your resurrection.*

The Lord's Prayer.